Ethnic Peace in
the American City

Ethnic Peace in the American City

Building Community in Los Angeles and Beyond

Edward T. Chang

and

Jeannette Diaz-Veizades

NEW YORK UNIVERSITY PRESS

New York and London

NEW YORK UNIVERSITY PRESS
New York and London

Library of Congress Cataloging-in-Publication Data
Chang, Edward T.
Ethnic peace in the American city : building community in Los
Angeles and beyond / Edward Chang and Jeannette Diaz-Veizades.
p.   cm.
Includes bibliographical references and index.
ISBN 0-8147-1583-4 (cloth : alk. paper)
ISBN 0-8147-1584-2 (pbk. : alk. paper)
1. Los Angeles (Calif.)—Ethnic relations. 2. Los Angeles
(Calif.)—Race relations. 3. Minorities—California—Los Angeles.
4. Riots—California—Los Angeles—History—20th century.
5. Community development—California—Los Angeles.   I. Diaz-Veizades,
Jeannette. II. Title.
F869.L89 A2517 1999
305.8'009794'94—dc21   99-6222
                    CIP

New York University Press books are printed on acid-free paper,
and their binding materials are chosen for strength and durability.

Manufactured in the United States of America

10 9 8 7 6 5 4 3 2 1

We dedicate this book to the residents of South Central, Pico-Union, and Koreatown.

Contents

Acknowledgments

This book is a culmination of several years of collaborative work. The University of California Academic Senates at Riverside supported our survey of Korean and Latino residents of Koreatown and Pico-Union. We especially thank Mr. Myung Ki Hong for the generous research funds for part of this research project.

The real work of building communities is the ongoing work of community-based organizations, churches, educators, and activists, work that requires a great deal of energy, creativity, wisdom, and vision. We would like to acknowledge the contribution of the Los Angeles Multicultural Collaborative for its groundbreaking work in Los Angeles and for its assistance in bringing together the Korean American and Central American community–based organizations who helped design the community survey presented in chapter 4. Specifically, we would like to thank Gary Phillips, Ruben Lizardo, Joe Hicks, and Marcia Choo for their unfailing passion and commitment to peace and justice. In addition, we express our appreciation to members of the Black Korean Alliance, the Latino Black Roundtable, and members of the African American community, Korean American community, and Latino and Central American communities who gave us their valuable time and opinions.

Many of our colleagues provided helpful suggestions and ideas for improving the research materials presented in this book. We would like to thank Charles Henry, Robert Blauner, Gerald Berreman, Ling Chi Wang, Elaine Kim, K. W. Lee, Chris Spies, and Nancy Cervantes.

Sojin Kim and Merril Gillespy provided invaluable editorial suggestions and corrections, and Jonathan Park helped us draw maps of Los Angeles and boundaries of ethnic communities. We also thank our family members (Angie, Janet, and Hadley) for their unconditional support, understanding, and patience.

Finally, grateful acknowledgment is made for granting permission to use sections of text from the following sources: "America's First Multiethnic Riots," in Karin Aguilar-San Juan, ed., *The State of Asian America: Activism and Resistance in the 1990s,* pp. 101–17 (Boston: South End Press, 1994); "Jewish and Korean Merchants in African American Neighborhoods: A Comparative Perspective," *Amerasian Journal* 19, no. 2 (November 1993): 5–21; "Building Cross-Cultural Coalitions: A Case Study of the Black Korean Alliance and the Latino Black Roundtable," *Ethnic and Racial Studies* 19, no. 3 (July 1996): 680–700; "African American Boycotts of Korean-Owned Stores in New York and Los Angeles," in Paul R. Brass, ed., *Riots and Pogroms,* pp. 235–52 (London: Macmillan, 1996).

Introduction
Building Multiethnic Communities

In recent years, racial tensions in Los Angeles and other major cities in the United States have increased amid changes in both the world economy and immigration patterns. Besides the long-standing conflictual relationship between African Americans and the traditional white majority, the dramatic demographic shifts in the last twenty years have polarized Los Angeles's many different ethnic and racial groups (e.g., Korean American–African American, Latino–African American, Asian–Latino, and white–African American). In the past two decades, neighborhoods in Los Angeles that were once predominantly African American have now become nearly half African American and half Latino. This change has been most noticeable in the south central area, where in 1980, the area's African American population was 66.7 percent and the Latino population 13.4 percent, but in 1990, the African American population had fallen to 48.9 percent and the Latino population had risen to 51 percent (Hayes-Bautista, Schink, and Hayes-Bautista 1993). South central Los Angeles is now where African Americans and Latinos live as neighbors and fellow job-seekers and Korean Americans own small businesses serving both African American and Latino customers.

Both the continuing discrimination in housing and the United States's changing labor force needs (such as the sharp decrease in manufacturing jobs) have put Latinos and African Americans in direct competition for housing, jobs, and access to educational and health institutions. Latinos and African Americans also compete politically: Latinos are demanding proportional representation to reflect the shift in population, and African Americans are trying to retain their share of political and economic gains to compensate for past injustices and also to strengthen their economic and political power. For example, three African American contractors filed an $800 million civil rights lawsuit against the city of Lynwood and

1

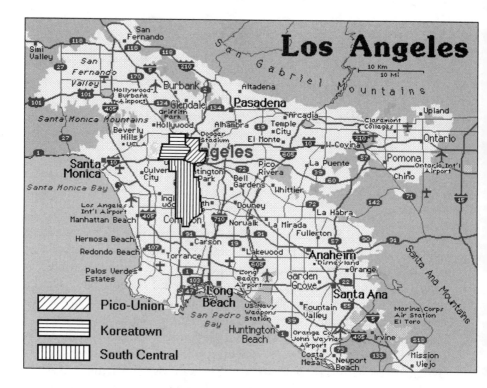

three Latino council members for discriminating against African American contractors (Leonard 1998, p. B3).[1]

The issues of resource, power, and job competition have intensified because the infrastructure of these inner-city neighborhoods has lagged far behind their ethnic transformation. The school system in Los Angeles is an excellent example: Just as the African American community was making inroads into the school system by training teachers and principals for positions of power, the faces of the children they were teaching suddenly turned from black to brown. Whereas white teachers had previously been looking into a sea of black faces, now black teachers are looking into a sea of brown faces. Overall, tensions between Latinos and African Americans in Los Angeles have cut across several dimensions (neighbor-neighbor, employer-employee, and employee-employee), as well as several different contexts (schools, social service facilities, and political institutions).

Historically, according to Omi and Winant (1986), the centrality of race in the United States has been based on a white-black paradigm; that is, problems of race have usually meant problems between blacks and whites. During the 1960s, "a riot ideology" gave black activists the political purpose of protesting the oppression of and discrimination against blacks in America (Brass 1996, p. 4). Then in the 1980s and 1990s, race and class debates again occupied the center stage in America, but in different forms. The heightened interethnic tensions among minority groups (i.e., Korean Americans and African Americans or African Americans and Latinos) underscored the complexity of race relations.

The theoretical and historical overemphasis on the black-white paradigm or two-group paradigm of race relations has led to a simplified understanding of intergroup relations; that is, there is not one path but many, not all of which converge in the same place. The dynamics between African Americans and white Americans are not the same as those between African Americans and Korean Americans or between Korean Americans and Central Americans. Rather, each of these pairings reflects unique differences in the intermixing of histories and cultures, and each of these groups holds distinctly different socioeconomic and sociopolitical positions vis-à-vis one another and society as a whole. It is the uniqueness of these intergroup dynamics that is overlooked when a black-white paradigm is used to understand the differences among ethnic communities. In addition, theoretical perspectives that do not simultaneously address issues of attitudes and perceptions, power disparities, the effects of demographic shifts, differences in culture and race, different histories of oppression and discrimination, and the position of racial conflict within the larger sociopolitical realm also cannot address the complexity of ethnic relations in multicultural urban centers like Los Angeles. The picture becomes even more complicated when we add the diversity within racial and ethnic groups, for example, the historical tensions between Japanese and Koreans or those between Mexicans and Central American groups or the class differences in any ethnic community.

To a greater extent than in nearly any other state, race relations in California have rarely if ever been defined solely along black-white lines. From the state's very beginning, race relations—often conflictual—have been between, or among, blacks, Latinos, Asians, whites, and Native Americans (Almaguer 1994, Calderon 1990, Chan 1986, Jackson 1991, Munoz and Henry 1990, Oliver and Johnson 1984, Takaki 1989). What is different about California today is the size of each ethnic group. Whites, traditionally considered to be the majority, are increasingly becoming a minority, and in many institutions and neighborhoods, no one ethnic group is in the clear numerical majority.[2] In particular, during the last two decades, the phenomenal growth of the Latino and Asian American populations has created a population both ethnically and economically diverse, which is a shift in demographics that has begun to change the perception of what it means to be a member of society (Ong 1994).

This struggle is particularly visible and poignant in Los Angeles, the primary gateway into the United States from both Latin American and Pacific Rim countries. According to *L.A. 2000: A City for the Future*, "Los Angeles will be the second largest consolidated metropolitan area in the United States with 18 million residents. More different races, religions, cultures, languages and people mingle here than any other city in the world" (1988). The problems associated with interactions among ethnic groups in rapidly changing political and economic structures was brought to the attention of the world with the so-called civil unrest in Los Angeles beginning on April 29, 1992. These riots, sparked by the acquittal of four white police officers implicated in the notorious Rodney King beating trial, not only marked a turning point in Los Angeles history but also awakened the nation to a new reality. This civil unrest forced the United States to reexamine the myth of the nation as a model multiethnic and multiracial society. Indeed, today, the myths of multiculturalism only disguise the sad reality of a society still "separate and unequal," and these misperceptions, conflicts, and tensions among minority groups are affecting the city's future. Accordingly, Los Angeles has emerged as a new laboratory for social scientists and human relations practitioners experimenting with and developing new ideas and policies concerning race relations in the United States. The city's rapid demographic shifts, coupled with equally rapid deindustrialization and a continually changing political landscape, make Los Angeles a rich and challenging place in which to analyze current race relations in the United States.

No consensus has emerged regarding the causes and meaning of the violence that erupted on April 29, 1992. The Korean American victims insist that the riots were targeted to their property. For many white Americans, the riots signaled the destruction of civil society in the city. Many African Americans prefer to use the term *rebellion* or *uprising* to refer to these events, to reflect their view that African Americans were protesting mainly against economic inequality and racial discrimination.

Numerous books, articles, newspaper articles, and commission reports on the 1992 Los Angeles riots/civil unrest have been published. For example, two collections (Baldassare 1994, Gooding-Williams 1993) present essays on the causes of the civil unrest written by various scholars, researchers, and activists; two commission reports investigated the causes of the Los Angeles riots and the role of the Los Angeles Police Department (LAPD) (McCone Commission Report 1965, Tucker 1992); and the *Los Angeles Times* published a detailed account of what happened on the fateful day of April 29, 1992: *Inside the L.A. Riots: What Really Happened and Why It Will Happen Again* (Institute for Alternative Journalism, 1992). In addition, many works analyze the unrest from the perspective of a particular ethnic group (e.g., Baldassare 1994, Gooding-Williams 1993, Madhubuti 1993).

Despite the numerous races and classes participating in the Los Angeles civil unrest, many scholars and many of the media continue to characterize the unrest in black and white terms. As *Los Angeles Times* columnist Bill Boyarsky wrote, "Despite the severity of Korean American losses, it seems most of the world views Los Angeles' racial troubles in terms of black and white" (1993, p. B1). But the Los Angeles civil unrest of 1992 clearly indicated that the analysis of race relations, and consequent interventions regarding race relations, must move beyond a black-white perspective (Baldassare 1994, Chang 1994a, Freer 1994, Min 1996, Park 1997, Torres 1995, Yoon 1997).

The notion that intergroup conflict often is centered on issues of unequal power and the distribution of resources is not new. At the same time, ethnic conflict contains its own misperceptions, and often one exacerbates the other. Indeed, it may be that at the root of any societal discontent and conflict are the perennial issues of resource scarcity and allocation and, ultimately, access to power and capital. At the grassroots, neighbor-to-neighbor level, economic and political competition is heightened by differences in cultural orientation and practices. These range from the most obvious differences in language, dress, food, and music to differences in household living patterns and political orientation (Tobas 1990).

A comparative understanding of Korean–African American and Korean-Latino relations may clarify interminority relations in the United States. Although the Los Angeles civil unrest of 1992 is an important historical reference for our book, we intend to focus more on the interaction and intersection between racial and ethnic groups (particularly Korean–African American and Latino–Korean American), coalition building, and the public policy implications for economic and demographic restructuring in America. In this way, we hope, first, to provide an empirical description of ethnic relations and dynamics among three racial groups in Los Angeles: African Americans and Korean Americans in south central Los Angeles, and Korean Americans and Latino Americans in the Pico-Union/Westlake area of Los Angeles. We hope, second, to use this description and understanding of racial relations between these groups to build communities in multicultural metropolitan areas.

With this in mind, in chapter 1 we review the historical, economic, and political reasons for civil unrest in the United States (focusing on Los Angeles), particularly the similarities and differences between the 1965 Watts riots and the 1992 civil unrest. Los Angeles's civil unrest in 1992 was dubbed "America's first multiethnic riots" because not only whites and African Americans but also Latinos, Central Americans, and Korean Americans were involved as both victims and assailants. We argue that the demographic and economic restructuring of the 1980s had a profound impact on racial and class relations that eventually contributed to the civil unrest in 1992.

Chapter 2 reviews theories of interethnic conflict and their applicability to current Korean–African American conflicts and analyzes Korean–African American conflict in the United States from psychological, cultural, economic, and ideological perspectives. Because the proliferation of Korean-owned stores in African American neighborhoods has heightened racial tensions between the two communities, our analysis of black-Korean relations in this chapter is based on interviews with 34 Korean businessmen in south central Los Angeles in 1988/89 and a survey of 165 African Americans and 178 Korean Americans conducted six to nine months after the April riots.

In chapter 3, we look at how the media, courts, politicians, and activists have manipulated the "facts" to inflame the conflict between Korean Americans and African Americans in Los Angeles and New York. We direct our discussion toward the influence of media on interethnic (i.e., Korean–African American) conflicts in Los Angeles and New York and argue that the mainstream media did indeed have a major role in creating the Korean–African American conflict. A comparative analysis of stories in the *Los Angeles Times* and the *New York Times* about conflicts between Korean merchants and African American community (1990/91) offers interesting insights into the media's part in constructing racial stereotypes, images, and perceptions and how they used these images to pit Korean merchants against African American residents.

Chapter 4 examines Korean-Latino relations in Los Angeles, specifically the Koreatown/Pico-Union area of Los Angeles, focusing on sociocultural, economic, and political issues. Whereas Korean–African American relations are primarily those between merchants and customers, Korean-Latino relations are multidimensional, between merchants and customers, employers and employees, worker and worker, and neighbor and neighbor. The relationship between Koreans and Latinos is continuing to develop in accordance with the impact of these two groups' recent immigration. Cheng and Espiritu (1989) proposed an "immigrant hypothesis" to explain the lack of conflict between Korean merchants and Latino customers and residents. Our study found that the interactions between Korean Americans and Latinos as merchant and customer, employer and employee, worker and worker, and neighbor and neighbor sometimes caused conflicts between the two groups. But our study also partially confirmed the "immigrant hypothesis," that many Latino and Korean immigrants share the same (hard) work ethic, willingness to sacrifice, and belief in American dreams. In fact, many of our survey's Latino respondents stated that they regarded Korean merchants as worthy of emulation. Likewise, as with African American and Korean American merchants in south central Los Angeles, relations between Central Americans and Korean Americans in Pico-Union and Koreatown reflect their psychological and cultural differences as well as their similar living conditions (fiscal neglect, underemployment, lack of educational resources, etc.) which often characterize poor and politically underrepresented communities. Like African Americans and Korean Americans, both Koreans and Latinos expressed a desire to improve their neighborhoods and to address their shared needs and concerns.

A case study of the Black-Korean Alliance (BKA) and the Latino-Black Roundtable (LBR) is the focus of chapter 5, which analyzes the establishment and demise of these two coalitions whose goals were to promote interethnic dialogue and communication. Through conversations with the coalitions' founding members and core participants, we explore the two groups' cultural differences, economic challenges, ethnic politics, and coalition dynamics. According to the coalition participants, "Talk alone was not enough." In concluding this chapter, we share some of the BKA and LBR members' visions of a multicultural Los Angeles.

In chapter 6, we redefine interethnic conflict resolution so as to link human relations approaches to community organizing and development approaches and describe the conflict resolution and community development practices of the South African ("Saamspan") model, which links mediation and conflict resolution to resource distribution, empowerment, and economic development based on models of justice and participatory democracy. Communities around the world are now asking whether it is possible for ethnically defined groups to live in cooperative harmony or whether they are doomed to continuously escalating ethnic friction.

1

America's First Multiethnic "Civil Unrest"

> We do not know very well what kind of society we live in, what kind of history we have had, what kind of people we are. We are just now beginning to find out, the hard way.
> —Richard E. Rubenstein and Robert Fogelson, eds.,
> *Mass Violence in America*

Racial and class tensions exploded into "civil unrest"[1] in Los Angeles on April 29, 1992. Television viewers were horrified by what they were seeing: a white truck driver, Reginald Denny, being beaten up by a group of young African American men at the corner of Normandie and Florence; a Latino man being beaten as he tried to rescue Denny; a Japanese American man being beaten while waiting at a bus stop. As smoke darkened the skies of Los Angeles, the issue of racism—in this "melting pot" of America—was brought to the forefront. The suspicion, fear, and distrust among ethnic and racial groups turned into a massive destruction of city neighborhoods.

Was what happened in April 1992 a riot or civil unrest? Some scholars have labeled it an uprising, insurrection, rebellion, or revolution, so perhaps it was a "political-protest-turned-into-riot" (Yu and Chang 1995). But even several years later, we still have not determined definitively what really happened on April 29, 1992, in Los Angeles. It is clear, however, that whatever it was did not result simply from the verdict in the highly publicized trial of the police officers who beat Rodney King. Rather, it was the culmination of years of neglect, abandonment, hopelessness, despair, alienation, injustice, isolation, and oppression of large segments of the city's population. The ensuing three days of terror and destruction left 52 people dead, 16,000 arrested, and nearly $1 billion in damaged or destroyed property. According to the Los Angeles County Sheriff's Department, 12,545 people were arrested between 6:00 P.M. on April 29 and 5:00 A.M. on May 5, 1992, of whom 45.2 percent were Latino, 41 percent African American, and 11.5 percent white (*Los Angeles Times*, May 21, 1992).[2]

Indeed, this could be said to be America's first multiethnic civil unrest (Chang 1995). According to Peter Kwong, "The fixation on black versus white is outdated and misleading—the Rodney King verdict was merely the match that lit the fuse of the first multiracial class riot in America" (1992, p. 29). Ruben Martinez noted how complex the picture of Los Angeles was in the aftermath of the 1992 riots:

> John Mack [of the Los Angeles branch of the Urban League] told Ted Koppel [of ABC's *Nightline*] that Korean Americans are in America now, and they have to learn in its ways. Korean Americans marching for peace on Saturday protested *Nightline*'s failure to include their voices. Latinos are eager to blame the unrest on blacks. And the city's Mexican-American leadership is virtually silent, unwilling or unable to deal with the Salvadoran problem in Pico Union. (Institute for Alternative Journalism 1992, p. 33)

Urban demographics have changed over the past twenty years, along with attitudes toward and perceptions of intergroup relations. Race relations can no longer be defined as a black-white issue, and many existing theories of race relations have become obsolete. There is thus an urgent need to develop new social and racial theories that take into account the rapidly changing demography of the United States, and several scholars (Almaguer 1994, Chang 1990, Diaz-Veizades and Chang 1996, Harris 1995, Torres 1995) are attempting to address racial relations using a multiracial and multiethnic approach.

The events beginning on April 29, 1992, reflected the development and complexity of the changing demography of Los Angeles, and they also were the inevitable outcome of the deteriorating living conditions of the residents of south central Los Angeles. If we look back at the Watts riots of 1965 and the intervening years up to April 1992, we can see how the social, economic, and racial dynamics in Los Angeles have changed—though not improved. It is interesting that although the root causes of the civil unrest have remained the same, the socioeconomic and political context has changed. More important, the demographic shift in both south central and greater Los Angeles has profoundly affected racial and ethnic relations.

Beyond Black and White

Although race relations often are analyzed in terms of a dominant white and a subordinate black population, America's policy on race was based on the early white settlers' encounters with Native Americans, and then on whites' relations with Asian Americans and Latinos (Almaguer 1994, Gossett 1965, Omi and Winant 1993). As Tomas Almaguer pointed out: "While longstanding race relations developed elsewhere were essentially binary in character, the United States' mid-nineteenth-century annexation of what is today the Southwest would incorporate three new cultural groups into existing racial patterns: the Mexican, Chinese, and Japanese populations" (1994, p. ix). For example, Native Americans were stereotyped as "uncivilized savages." Asians were denied meaningful participation in American political processes and even due process of the law, because they were considered "aliens" not eligible to become naturalized citizens (Chan 1991, Hing 1993, Takaki 1989).

Omi and Winant's notion of "racial formation" is a useful concept for understanding the fluidity of racial and ethnic categorization in America: "The meaning of race is defined and contested throughout society, in both collective and personal practice. In the process, racial categories themselves are formed, transformed, destroyed and re-formed. Therefore, racialization is an ideological process, and a historically specific one"(Omi and Winant 1986, p. 61). Furthermore, the "ethnicity" factor shapes not only domestic policies but also the United States's foreign policy (DeConde 1992). DeConde argued that "ethnoracial affiliation" played a critical role in formulating America's foreign policy decision-making process. For example, even though Liberia became an independent state in 1847, the United States was the last of the Western nations to establish normal diplomatic relations with the new African country (DeConde 1992, p. 40). During the Falkland Islands War between Britain and Argentina (1982), Anglo-American loyalty was responsible for providing unconditional support to Britain, even though the American government maintained friendly relations with Argentina as well (DeConde 1992, pp. 184–85).

Ethnic and economic restructuring in America has further polarized the population along racial and class lines, and in Los Angeles, the sharp increase in the Latino and Asian populations has profoundly altered the city's face over the past two decades. The passage in 1965 of the Immigration and Naturalization Act abolished the discriminatory policy favoring immigrants from western Europe and established an open system based on reunifying families and designed to ensure that no country would be given special preferences or quotas (Hing 1993). This reform led to significant population changes in the country's major metropolitan areas, and as a result, the majority of immigrants to the United States today come from Asia and Latin America. In addition, affluent white and minority groups have moved from the inner city to the suburbs, causing the proportion of whites in Los Angeles County to decline from 52.4 percent in 1980 to 46.3 percent in 1988. In an article in the *Los Angeles Times*, Gerald Horne commented on the changing dynamics of race relations in America: "The black-white dyad has not been as prominent historically and, to a certain extent, has been overshadowed by racial issues relating to Native Americans, Mexican Americans and Asian Americans" (1997, p. M1).

Los Angeles has become a truly multiracial and multiethnic city. According to the 1990 census, 40 percent of its population is Latino, 37 percent white, 13 percent African American, 9 percent Asian American, and 1 percent Native American. Not surprisingly, the impact of demographic changes on the ethnic and racial composition of the Los Angeles Unified School District (LAUSD) between 1967 and 1987 is striking. From 1967 to 1977 to 1987, the proportion of white students dropped from 54.6 to 33.7 to 16.7 percent. In contrast, the proportion of Hispanic students increased from 19.4 to 56.7 percent during the same period, and the proportion of Asian and Pacific Islander students also jumped from 3.9 percent in 1967 to 8.3 percent in 1987. This racial and ethnic recomposition heightened racial tensions and increased the incidence of violence. Conflicts between Latino and African American students at local schools have broken out several times in the past few years. At Inglewood High School, African American and Latino students have clashed repeatedly, feeling that the campus administration favored one group over the other in approving and supporting certain events. The number of reported hate crimes also has increased sharply. During the 1992/93 school year, 383 students in elementary, junior high, and high school were assaulted with deadly weapons, and the Los Angeles County Human Relations Commission's study of intergroup conflict notes that more than 354 schools reported hate crimes against students or employees in that one-year period (Multicultural Collaborative 1996, pp. 56, 54).

Since the civil unrest of 1992, Los Angeles has had to deal with a new set of challenges, in which two opposite trends are noteworthy. One is the polarization and fragmentation of the city's population along racial and ethnic lines, and the other trend is the mobilization of new groups that previously were outside the political process. With different racial groups vying for employment opportunities, health care, social services, and political representation, the potential for conflict is never far away. It thus was not surprising that the city's political response to the riots only opened wider the rifts among ethnic and racial groups.

Watts and South Central Los Angeles

In 1965, south central Los Angeles was largely known as a "black area" that was 81 percent African American. But during the past two and half decades, the demographics of south central Los Angeles have radically shifted, and now nearly 50 percent of the residents of south central Los Angeles are Latino. The face of south central Los Angeles has changed as the black flight to the suburbs accelerated during the 1980s. Between 1980 and 1990, the African American population of south central Los Angeles fell 20 percent, from 369,504 to 295,312. During the same period, the African American population of the nearby Inland Empire of Riverside and San Bernardino Counties increased by 99 percent and 134 percent, respectively.

The history of the African American community in Los Angeles began in the late nineteenth and early twentieth century when many blacks from the South moved to Southern California, lured by promises of inexpensive homes, ample business opportunities, and relatively lower levels of discrimination (Bunch 1992, de Graaf 1962).

African American migration to Los Angeles and California took place in three waves: between 1870 and 1930, the decade of the 1930s, and between 1942 and 1950. Numerous obstacles hampered African American migration to Southern California during the early period: First, transportation problems (rough roads and expenses) discouraged blacks from moving to Los Angeles. Second, because of racial discrimination, few industrial jobs were open to black and other nonwhite workers. Third, labor unions, nativist groups, and employer associations strongly opposed the migration of nonwhites to California. Last, the Mexicans and Asians already living in California provided an ample supply of cheap labor for California's agriculture industry.

Nonetheless, the warm climate and employment opportunities created by World War I attracted many African Americans to California, and unlike many other groups, they came to Los Angeles as individuals, without help from any organizational networks in the African American community (Collins 1980, p. 9). Although blacks in Los Angeles experienced some degree of discrimination in housing and employment, they were able to secure work in the unskilled labor market at wages much higher than anywhere else in the nation. Furthermore, compared with other regions, African Americans faced less hostility because Californians were much more concerned with curbing the increasing number of Asian immigrants than the small number of blacks from the South. In fact, African Americans enjoyed a reduction in racial tension and a degree of acceptance while at the same time, Chinese immigrants were being excluded from jobs and driven from many cities. By 1910, 35 percent of African Americans in Los Angeles owned their own homes, compared with 2.4 percent in New York City and 14.1 percent in Dallas (Bunch 1992). In fact, by 1920, there were more than eighty-six black-owned businesses on Central Avenue—symbols of the burgeoning dreams of the African American community (Oliver and Johnson 1984). The relative prosperity of the African American community was such that the early 1900s were labeled the "Golden Era," said to be paralleled only by the cultural renaissance occurring simultaneously in New York's Harlem.

This does not mean, however, that the blacks in Los Angeles did not face social segregation and employment discrimination. The growing influence of the Ku Klux Klan and heightened racial fears from 1910 to 1920 resulted in racially biased housing restrictions. These restrictions, combined with the continued influx of African Americans into Los Angeles, laid the foundation for the pattern of racial segregation and the creation of ghettos that still exist in Los Angeles today. Institutionalized housing discrimination and racial segregation and the practice of restrictive covenants forced new residents to settle in areas already overcrowded with African Americans. The rapid growth of the population, coupled with residential segregation, made the African American district even more congested, and the shortage of housing persisted. By 1940, nearly 70 percent of blacks resided in the 45–square-mile area known today as south central Los Angeles (de Graaf 1962).

The 1940s and World War II brought with them the industrialization of Southern California and a population explosion in the area as people came looking for work after the lean years of the Great Depression. In the spring and summer of 1942, the tremendous growth in industrial plants and the chronic labor shortage during World War II opened defense jobs to African Americans. These opportunities attracted a new wave of blacks to California, and many found jobs in shipbuilding and aircraft plants and the rubber industry. But African Americans continued to suffer from discriminatory hiring and promotion practices. As Collins pointed out, "While opportunities were often in janitorial and menial jobs, nearly all clerical and commercial jobs in private firms were closed to African Americans" (1980, p. 24).

In the summer of 1964, riots broke out in African American communities in seven cities in the eastern United States (McCone Commission 1965, p. 2).[3] Then a year later, on a hot summer day, south central Los Angeles exploded as rioters set fires and looted liquor stores, furniture stores, clothing stores, department stores, and pawn shops. This continued for six days, during which time 34 persons were killed, 1,032 were injured, and 3,952 were arrested (Rubenstein and Fogelson 1969, p. 147). Around 200 buildings were damaged by fire or looted, damage that in today's dollars would be a staggering $183 million (*Los Angeles Times,* May 21, 1992, p. 10). Twenty-seven years later, the city of Los Angeles again erupted in violence and flames. The Tucker Committee's report summarized the consequences and implications: "The three-days of destruction left 52 dead, countless injured, and $750 million in property damaged or destroyed. The city that prided itself on its diversity had become the site of the worst multiethnic urban conflict in the United States history" (Tucker Committee 1992, p. 1). Before we examine the similarities and differences between the Watts riot of 1965 and the Los Angeles civil unrest of 1992, we will look at the historical development of Watts and south central Los Angeles.

Before World War II, "the city of Watts prospered and remained predominantly a middle class district of professional, white collar workers and government employees" (Collins 1980, p. 42). Then, between 1940 and 1950, the existing African American district expanded farther south to the Watts area to accommodate the large influx of migrants, most of whom could not afford to settle anywhere else. By providing jobs and transportation to the area's residents, the Pacific Electric Railroad Company greatly influenced the development of Watts. But it was not able to handle the large influx of migrants in such a short period of time, and it began to deteriorate, owing to housing shortages, transportation problems, increasing crime, inadequate medical care, and, particularly, employment discrimination. Watts became a lower-class community of mainly African American residents.

Although the African American migrants had been attracted initially by employment opportunities, once they arrived, many found themselves unemployed or underemployed. Even World War II and the industrial expansion in Los Angeles brought little improvement; institutional discrimination and overt racism prevented African Americans from realizing their California dreams. For example, African Americans were not allowed to join labor unions, and as a result, they could find only low-paying, unskilled, or temporary employment. In addition, those able to find defense-related employment (skilled or semiskilled) were the first employees fired when defense production tapered off.

The end of World War II put many African Americans out of work with the closing of war-related manufacturing plants and the return of (white) soldiers from the battlefront. According to Collins, "Between the hours of 8:00 A.M. and 5:00 P.M., Watts was 90 percent white and between the hours of 5:00 P.M. and 6:00 A.M., Watts was 90 percent African American" (1980, p. 49). By the 1950s, Watts and south central Los Angeles resembled a "ghetto" suffering from chronic poverty, a high unemployment rate, inferior schooling, and a high school-dropout rate. In fact, the unemployment rate in south central Los Angeles was two to three times higher than that of the surrounding communities. Thus it was the combination of housing shortages, underemployment and unemployment, poor community relations with the police, and the general fiscal neglect of the inner city that resulted in the Watts riot of 1965 (McCone Commission 1965). In the aftermath of the Watts riots, those in the community who could leave the area did, taking with them professional and capital resources, the loss of which only made it more difficult to rebuild (Bunch 1992, Case 1972).

Despite the lessons of the Watts riot, the socioeconomic conditions of south central Los Angeles continued to deteriorate during the next twenty years. Indeed, 1990 census data show that the living conditions of African Americans in Watts have worsened since the 1960s, with the 1990 poverty rate at 30.3 percent, compared with 27 percent at the time of the Watts riots. Also in 1990, the per capita income of south central Los Angeles was $7,023, compared with $16,149 for Los Angeles County as a whole. More important, half of those aged sixteen and older were neither employed nor looking for jobs. Clearly, the economic recovery and boom of 1980s did not help improve economic conditions for the residents of Watts and south central Los Angeles. Instead, African American residents in poor neighborhoods often have to pay a "black tax," that is, higher insurance and mortgage interest rates, abusive police, and lower-quality schools. By most indicators (e.g., employment levels, access to housing and social services, police-community relations), conditions existing even before the 1965 Watts riots gave rise to the 1992 civil unrest.

The Emergence of the New South Central Los Angeles

Before the 1980s, General Motors, Goodyear, Firestone, and Bethlehem Steel were major sources of jobs and economic security for the residents of south central Los Angeles. But by the 1980s, all these plants had vanished from the area (Institute for Alternative Journalism 1992, p. 144).[4] In a study of racial inequality in Los Angeles, Ong and his colleagues found that "in the late 1970s and early 1980s alone, Los Angeles lost more than 50,000 industrial jobs to plant closures in the auto, tire, steel and non-defense aircraft industries. Since 1971, south central Los Angeles, the core of the African American community, itself lost 321 firms."[5]

African Americans also worry that they are losing the political and economic "gains" they made as a result of the 1960s civil rights struggle. Because south central Los Angeles has now become a multiethnic community, blacks are becoming increasingly concerned that they are losing influence and control in what used to be their "exclusive" domain and are often suspicious and resentful of the growing numbers of Latino immigrants and Asians (i.e., Korean) in "their own neighborhoods." Latino and African American communities are already arguing over the city council's redistricting plan, employment opportunities, and economic justice in Los Angeles. For example, whereas Latinos are demanding proportional representation to reflect the changes in population, African Americans insist that they are entitled to retain their share of the gains that were meant to compensate for past injustices.

In the meantime, Asian Americans are beginning to participate in the political process. For example, after April 1992, the Korean American Victims Association staged protests every day in front of city hall to demand compensation for Korean business owners who lost their businesses during the riots, a move that signaled the increasing politicization of this immigrant community.

A Brief History of Korean Immigration to the United States

Although Koreans began immigrating to the United States at the turn of the century, until recently Korean Americans had been an "invisible minority." But since the Los Angeles civil unrest of 1992, Korean Americans have emerged as one of the most visible ethnic groups in the United States. One reason is that a disproportionately high number of Korean American–owned stores were destroyed during the riots. Another reason is the rapid growth of the Korean American population in the United States during the past two decades. In fact, according to 1990 census data, Koreans were the fastest-growing Asian population in the United States between 1970 and 1990. In real numbers, the Korean population in the United States increased 412 percent, from 70,000 to 354,593, of which 82 percent were foreign born. Between 1980 and 1990, the Korean American population increased 125 percent, to 798,849. Following this trend, the Korean American population of Los Angeles also has grown, rising from 60,618 in 1980 to 145,431 in 1990. In fact, since the 1970s, Los Angeles has been the home of the largest Korean community in the United States and is one of the few cities in this country that has officially recognized the geographical area known as "Koreatown."

Korean immigrants differ from other Asian immigrants in that many of them are Christians, and the Protestant church has been and still is the dominant and most influential institution in the Korean American community. These churches are not only places to worship but also centers of social, cultural, economic, and political activities.

After the liberalization of the immigration and naturalization laws—particularly after changes in the immigration quotas in the 1965—thousands of Korean immigrants have been settling in the United States. According to the 1990 census, the proportion of foreign-born Korean Americans was 80 percent, and in addition, the post-1965 Korean immigrants differ greatly from the earlier newcomers. At first, many of them were from urban areas, highly educated, professionals, and middle class, and so they were commonly known as "new urban immigrants." Yu, Yang, and Phillips found that in 1975, 65 percent of Korean immigrants were from professional or managerial backgrounds but that in 1977 this figure had dropped to 50 percent (1982, p. 51). Then during the 1980s and 1990s, Yoon (1997) found that the occupations of recent Korean immigrants had changed, specifically that (1) the proportion of professional workers had steadily decreased, (2) the proportion of white-collar workers in managerial, sales, and clerical occupations had steadily increased, and (3) the proportion of manual laborers, farmers, and service workers had increased. All these changes were a result of the growing role of family networks and changes in U.S. immigration policy.

Although the proportion of highly educated and professional Korean immigrants is declining, it is still considerably higher than that of any other group, including whites. For example, of recent Korean immigrant males twenty-five years and older, 52 percent have a bachelor's degree or higher, compared with 22 percent for white Americans. In addition, the newest Korean immigrants come as a family unit, whereas most of the earlier Koreans were young, single, and male. According to Yu and colleagues, "A typical Korean family in California is composed of parents and children, a structure that constitutes 61 percent of the total families" (1982, p. 44). The same study found that one-half the Korean families in Los Angeles have two or three children, an important fact, since many Korean store owners use their children as a source of cheap or unpaid labor. Indeed, Light and Bonacich found that "one-third of Korean American entrepreneurs reported some use of unpaid workers" (1988, p. 179), presumably family members.

Since 1965, economic and educational opportunities seem to have been the two most important reasons for Koreans to immigrate to the United States. Economic security seems to supersede even the education of Korean immigrant children, and many Korean entrepreneurs work twelve to sixteen hours a day at their small, mom-and-pop stores, 365 days a year. As a result, many Korean youth are battling adjustment problems, peer pressure, language difficulties, and culture shock. One of the main reasons for the rise of juvenile delinquency among Korean youth is the lack of parental supervision or guidance, with many immigrant parents simply too busy trying to make a living to spend time with their children.

Other Koreans came to America to escape the fear of attack from North Korea or military dictatorship and political instability in South Korea. The military, economic, and political ties between the United States and South Korea also induced large numbers of urban middle-class Koreans to emigrate. For these reasons, the new urban immigrants tend to be highly motivated, Westernized, individualistic, and materialistic, traits that may explain the high risk–taking behavior of Korean immigrant entrepreneurs before the Los Angeles civil unrest of 1992. For example, during the 1980s, Koreans were one of the few ethnic groups willing to open businesses in the high-crime areas of south central Los Angeles. As a result, tensions between the Korean immigrant merchants and African American residents throughout the United States increased during the 1980s and 1990s. Furthermore, professional, middle-class Korean immigrants usually bring enough investment capital with them to start small businesses immediately. According to Illsoo Kim, these resources (education, motivation, and money) are responsible for both the proliferation and the "success" of Korean enterprise (Kim 1981).

A Brief History of Latino Immigration to Los Angeles

Asians and Latinos are currently the two fastest-growing populations in the United States (Hing 1993). Between 1970 and 1980, the Latino population of the United States grew by 61 percent, and today it continues to grow by at least five times the rate of the non-Latino population (Fuchs 1991). More than 40 percent of the population of Los Angeles is Latino, many of whom are first-generation immigrants (Hurtado 1992). Whereas in 1960, Mexican-born Angelenos made up only 2 percent of the entire population, by 1990, Mexican immigrants accounted for 27 percent of the region's population and 33 percent of those living in Los Angeles County.

The Mexican population of Los Angeles differs from many of the other immigrant and cultural groups in the area, in that it is a mix of recent arrivals and already established families. According to the 1990 census, 3.7 million people in Los Angeles are of Mexican origin, 46 percent of whom were born abroad. Natives of the area are primarily the children of those born in Mexico, plus a relatively small number of second- and third-generation adults. Contrary to common misperception, much of the growth of Los Angeles County's Latino population is not due to recent immigration but, rather, to natural population increases (i.e., the number of live births minus the number of deaths).

Because of the high birthrates, the Latino population tends to be young compared with other ethnic groups. As discussed in chapter 4, a youthful population makes more demands on community resources in regard to day care, education, and employment. Although the majority of Latinos in Los Angeles are of Mexican origin, Central Americans are gaining prominence as well. The majority of Salvadoran and Guatemalan immigrants in the United States end up living in California. According to a report prepared by the Tomas Rivera Center, 52 percent of Guatemalans and 49 percent of Salvadorans counted in the 1990 census reside in Los Angeles, and the three largest Central American immigrant groups there are Salvadorans (302,000), Guatemalans (159,000), and Nicaraguans (44,000). These numbers reflect nearly a fivefold increase from the 1980 population (Lopez, Poppin, and Telles 1995). Less than 3 percent of the Salvadoran and Guatemalan residents in Los Angeles were born in the United States.

The Central American immigrants in Los Angeles are scattered throughout the city. Even in the Hollywood and Pico-Union areas, which contain the largest number of Salvadorans and Guatemalans, Central Americans are not a numerical majority, and neither area contains the bulk of the Los Angeles–based Salvadoran and Guatemalan population. Furthermore, less than 10 percent of the Salvadoran and Guatemalan population of Los Angeles County live in the Pico-Union/Westlake area. For the most part, Central Americans live in neighborhoods that provide inexpensive housing but not easy access to public transportation (Rodriguez and Vasquez-Rodriguez 1993).

Whereas Mexican immigrants most often come to the United States for economic reasons, Central American immigrants usually come for political reasons, to escape civil strife and oppression in their home countries. Accordingly, a large percentage of Central American immigrants in the United States, particularly the children, bear emotional and psychological scars, as many of them have witnessed, or personally experienced, the mutilation, torture, and/or disappearance of family members; killings; massacres of entire communities; bombings; and relocations. The following narrative is typical of the experience of Central American immigrants:

> Carmen Quinones arrived in Los Angeles for the first time in March 1976. She paid for the trip with money she received as compensation for her father's accidental death as a longshoreman in El Salvador. Planning to remain in the United States for only two years, she made the trip alone, leaving behind her mother and two daughters. The first leg of her trek was by bus to Tijuana with the first of three "coyotes." A second coyote helped her cross the Mexican-U.S. border; a third drove her to a cousin's home in Los Angeles. Predictably, the two years Quinones believed she would be away turned into three, then four. Five and a half years later she returned to her family.

During her absence one of her brothers had been murdered. "They say he was killed by a death squad," said Quinones. "Their faces were covered. They probably thought he was a guirrilero." But he wasn't. A few months after she arrived in El Salvador, armed men wearing masks invaded her home again. "Five men came to the house looking for my older brother and began spraying the house with bullets. We were all told to lie on the floor, face down, with our arms extended. My brother and a couple of aunts were there. My brother was in the airport at the time trying to track down a package. They never found him. I became very afraid and the next day began making arrangements to leave. Things had gotten very bad while I was away." (Delgado 1993, pp. 1–3)

The story of Carmen Quinones can be retold over and over again by the thousands of Salvadorans who fled the terror of their country's civil war only to find themselves in rat-infested, overcrowded living quarters in violent neighborhoods where neither they nor their children are safe. It is no wonder that many Salvadorans in Los Angeles felt that they were once again in the heart of the civil war when the streets of Los Angeles erupted into fire in April 1992.

The root of Salvadoran and Guatemalan immigration in political violence has resulted in an immigrant group with characteristics distinctly different from those immigrant groups who came to the United States for principally economic reasons. Korean immigrants, for example, brought with them social and economic capital, including managerial and entrepreneurial experience and relatively extensive education, whereas Salvadoran and Guatemalan immigrants brought with them little educational or capital resources. In fact, Salvadoran and Guatemalan immigrants come with fewer years of schooling than do other Latin and Central American immigrant groups.

Another defining characteristic of Salvadoran and Guatemalan immigrants is that they have the largest percentage of undocumented immigrants than any other cultural group in the United States. According to the U.S. Immigration and Naturalization Services, the rate of unauthorized immigration from 1990 to 1992 was about twice the rate indicated by census figures for the late 1980s. Unofficial 1992 figures for Salvadoran and Guatemalan immigrants in Los Angeles are 178,000 and 80,000, respectively (Chinchilla and Hamilton 1997). This large percentage of undocumented immigrants makes Salvadorans and Guatemalans perhaps the most vulnerable immigrant community in Los Angeles, their vulnerability increased by the fact that they often are poor and work in marginal sectors of the economy.

Salvadoran and Guatemalan immigrants to the United States have not, on the whole, been greatly welcomed. Although many came through Mexico without documentation, 97 percent of Salvadorans and 90 percent of Guatemalans who did apply for asylum during the 1980s were turned down (Jonas 1996). Salvadorans obtained temporary refuge status when the 1990 ABC class action suit and the 1991 Temporary Protected Status (TPS) were passed, the TPS program was ended in 1995, leaving 187,000 Salvadorans with only nine months to find alternative ways to legalize their status. Guatemalans were never given the protection that the TPS program offered to Salvadorans. The undocumented status of many Central Americans has made them a highly exploitable labor force, not only in agriculture, but also in the garment industry's sweatshops, which, ironically, are often run by Korean immigrants.

Despite these hardships, in their survey of Central American immigrants in Los Angeles, Chinchilla and Hamilton (1997) found that nearly 50 percent have chosen to stay in the area. Their principal reason is that employment in the United States provides income for family members remaining in the home country. Indeed, the money sent from immigrants in the United States to El Salvador and Guatemala has become a bulwark of security for families in these countries and is estimated, respectively, at $1 billion and $500,000 each year (Jonas 1996). Increasingly, Central American immigrants are coming to the United States for economic rather than political reasons, and the continued economic instability of the Central American countries helps ensure a steady flow.

The Central Americans have a long history of political organizing, which is reflected in the work of groups such as the Central American Resource Center (CARECEN) and the Coalition for Humane Immigrant Rights in Los Angeles (CHIRLA) to obtain licenses for street vendors.[6] By building alliances between African Americans and Latinos, by educating the public about the role of street vendors, these two community organizations succeeded in legalizing street vending in Los Angeles. The Sidewalk Vending Coalition of Los Angeles (SVC-LA) continues to work to protect the rights of street vendors.

Civil Unrest in Los Angeles, 1965 and 1992

What occurred in Los Angeles in the summer of 1965 and again in the spring of 1992 have many similarities. Indeed, the following description of the Watts riots could be easily be mistaken for an account of the Los Angeles riots of 1992:

> They looted stores, set fires, beat up white passersby whom they hauled from stopped cars, many of which were turned upside down and burned, exchanged shots with law enforcement officers, and stoned and shot at firemen. The rioter seemed to have been caught up in an insensate rage of destruction. (Special Advisor 1992, p. 1)

Another disturbing consequence of both incidents was the tripling of gun sales. During the Watts riot, "some pawnshops and gun stores have been robbed of firearms and gun sales reportedly have tripled since the riots." (Kerner Commission 1988, p. 153).

Numerous studies, commissions, and investigations were undertaken to try to identify the "causes" of the riots. The McCone Commission's report (1965) concluded that the major contributing factors of the Watts riots were a lack of jobs, poor schools, and hatred of police. The Kerner Commission's report (1988) found that pervasive discrimination and segregation in employment, and education were the major "causes" of race riots during the 1960s in America.[7] The California State Assembly Special Committee's report (1992) stated that "we are not the first official body formed to examine the causes of urban unrest; we may only hope that we are the last" (Tucker Committee 1992, p. 8). These studies and reports generally suggest that structural deficiencies and the economic disparity between whites and blacks were the main contributing factors to the race riots in Los Angeles as well as to those in other cities in the United States. The Tucker Committee concluded that

> little has changed in 1992 Los Angeles. . . . The Committee finds the causes of the 1992 unrest were the same as the causes of the unrest of the 1960's, aggravated by a highly visible increasing concentration of wealth at the top of the income scale and a decreasing Federal and State commitment to urban programs serving those at the bottom of the income scale. (Tucker Committee 1992, pp. 10, 13)[8]

The Kerner Commission warned that America was moving toward two separate societies, one black and one white, separate and unequal. Twenty years later, Hacker made a similar assessment of white-black relations in his book *Two Nations: Black and White, Separate, Hostile, Unequal* (1992). The Los Angeles civil unrest of 1992 was sparked by the verdicts in the Rodney King case, but the mass looting was rooted in the economic conditions of south central Los Angeles. In regard to the changing racial and ethnic dynamics, the Assembly Special Committee on the Los Angeles Crisis noted that "Los Angeles is also moving towards a society divided by race—yet the fault lines here will be drawn in black, brown, yellow and white. No American city has ever faced the task of providing economic opportunity and a climate of mutual tolerance for so many different ethnic groups" (Institute for Alternative Journalism 1992, p. 13). Many questions about the violence that erupted in 1965 and 1992 in Los Angeles remain unanswered. Was there a preestablished plan for the rioting in Watts? Was there a conspiracy to riot before the Rodney King trial verdicts were announced? The McCone Commission's report concluded that "there is no evidence of a pre-plan or a pre-established central direction of the rioting activities. This is not to say that there was no agitation or promotion of the rioting by local groups or gangs which exist in pockets throughout the south central area" (McCone Commission 1965, p. 22). Many observers suspect that the 1992 Los Angeles civil unrest was highly organized and planned ahead of time by gang members. However, an FBI investigation of the Los Angeles riots could not find any concrete evidence to support these suspicions. Charles J. Parsons, the FBI special agent in charge, added, "I am not ruling out the possibility that there was pre-rioting plan, but we don't have any hard evidence of that" (*Los Angeles Times*, July 25, 1992).

There are several important differences between the Watts riots and the Los Angeles riots. The Los Angeles riots were a multiethnic uprising that encompassed not only south central Los Angeles but also the Pico-Union and Koreatown areas, whereas the Watts riots were primarily a revolt by blacks against injustice and racism and were confined to the south central part of the city. Therefore, the Watts riots can be framed more easily in terms of binary relations between the dominant white and the subordinate black populations, compared with the multiethnic civil unrest of 1992.

The Consequences of Civil Unrest

In the past, race riots in America have usually been very localized. For example, the looting and burning during the Watts riots were limited to south central Los Angeles. The Los Angeles riots of 1992, in contrast, quickly spread beyond south central Los Angeles into Koreatown, downtown, Hollywood, Pico-Union, and even to west-side middle-class neighborhoods. Koreatown and Korean merchants in south central Los Angeles suffered the most damage during the riots. According to the Association of Korean American Victims, more than 2,280 Korean-owned businesses were looted, partially burned, or totally destroyed, costing approximately $400 million in damages.[9] According to a survey conducted eleven months after the riots, almost 40 percent of Korean Americans said that they were thinking of leaving Los Angeles (Kang 1993b, p. B1). Another study found that more than 50 percent of Korean businessmen were facing a "very difficult" financial situation (Rivera 1992, p. A3). Finally, a survey conducted by the Korean American InterAgency Council (KAIAC) found that 15 percent of Korean American college-age youth had dropped out of school because of the riots (Kang 1993c, p. B3).

Los Angeles's Latino community, particularly the Pico-Union district, also suffered major damages. A study published by the Tomas Rivera Center found that "Latinos were among those seriously affected by the uprising and also among those least served by the emergency response from private and public agencies (Pastor 1993, p. 4). The same study found that 30 percent of those who died were Latino and that up to 40 percent of the damaged businesses were owned by Latinos.

The public's reaction to the riots in 1965 and the 1992 also were different. In the 1960s, the civil rights movement gained momentum, and many Americans, including whites, were sympathetic to the issues of poverty, racism, unemployment, and injustice and were willing to provide assistance to improve the quality of life for African Americans and other disadvantaged minorities. In contrast, however, with the rise of the neoconservative movement in America during the late 1970s and 1980s, white Americans in 1992 were no longer willing to "pay for" social and economic programs to aid underprivileged "minorities." The Los Angeles civil unrest of 1992 also has been characterized as a "bread riot." One woman who participated in the looting explained that "this was the first time she could get shoes for all six of her children at once." In sum, several factors contributed to the frustration and worsening living conditions for the residents of south central Los Angeles: deindustrialization, the rise of neoconservatism, dissatisfaction with law enforcement and the justice system, and the arrival of Latino immigrants and Asian merchants. When these factors became overwhelming, the riots were the result.

The Deindustrialization of America and the Widening Gap among Classes

The recent deindustrialization and relocation of American firms have hurt the African American community. Many American corporations have shut down their manufacturing plants in the United States in order to relocate abroad (often in Asia or Mexico), where cheaper labor enables lower production costs. This structural realignment of the American economy during the 1970s and 1980s was the United States's response to the economic crisis created by increasing global competition. "Runaway shops" and overseas investment were the aggressive tactics used by capitalists to regain competitiveness and increase profits. By the early 1980s, "every newscast seemed to contain a story about a plant shutting down, another thousand jobs disappearing from a community, or the frustrations of workers unable to find full-time jobs utilizing their skills and providing enough income to support their families" (Bluestone and Harrison 1982, p. 4). Although some politicians blamed the greater number of imports from Asia for the loss of American jobs, it was the deindustrialization of the U.S. economy that caused the plant closures and the loss of American jobs. It has been estimated that during the 1970s, private disinvestments in plants and equipment eliminated at least 32 million jobs in the United States (Bluestone and Harrison 1982, p. 35). In addition, many companies simply decided to move to other areas where wages were lower, unions weaker, and the business climate better. Because of these developments, however, unemployment was no longer the problem of the poor; middle-class workers in traditional manufacturing industries such as steel, rubber, and automobiles were the hardest hit when they were permanently laid off with no prospect of finding equivalent employment.

This deindustrialization, not surprisingly, worsened the socioeconomic conditions of south central Los Angeles. The Tucker Committee reported that "the Los Angeles area lost more than 300,000 jobs between

June 1990 and February 1992, accounting for 60 percent of the statewide job losses during the period. The regional losses exacerbated the employment crisis in areas such as south central Los Angeles" (1992, p. 11). Despite the warning of the Kerner Commission in 1968 that America was headed toward two separate and unequal societies—one white and the other black—the gap between the haves and the have-nots only widened during the 1970s and 1980s (Bluestone and Harrison 1982, Ong et al., 1989, Phillips 1991). The report by the Milton S. Eisenhower Foundation, which was released in conjunction with the thirtieth anniversary of the Kerner Commission's report, stated that "the prediction has come to pass, in large part because poverty has become entrenched in the nation's inner cities, creating a cycle of crime, lack of education, unemployment and hopelessness" (*Los Angeles Times*, March 1, 1998, p. A18).

The Neoconservative Era of the 1980s

Many people believe that the Los Angeles riots of 1992 were an inevitable consequence of the failed neoconservative policies of the 1980s. Two decades before then, in 1964, the Civil Rights Act and the Immigration Act were passed, but after that, the Republican Party captured the presidency of the United States with strong support from white middle-class voters. Beginning with the landmark *Bakke* decision (1975), the attitudes of white Americans began to shift from progressive (a willingness to support social and economic programs to aid minorities) to conservative (a desire to reduce taxes, an emphasis on morality and strong family values, the repeal of affirmative action, and law and order) views.[10] Allan Bakke, a white applicant to the University of California at Davis's medical school, argued that the university's special admissions program that set aside "quotas" for blacks, Mexican Americans, and Asian Americans had wrongly discriminated against him. The U.S. Supreme Court ruled in Bakke's favor and thereby abolished the special admissions programs at the University of California campuses. The Court's ruling led the way to ending the racial programs and policies established in the 1960s to correct past injustice against racial minorities. These neoconservative public policies abolishing social programs left thousands of inner-city residents in a state of despair and hopelessness and excluded them from the prosperity of the 1980s economic boom.

During the 1980s, the conservative political climate enabled the social programs for inner cities to be drastically cut, with many white Americans demonstrating through their votes that they were more willing to spend their tax dollars on defense than on so-called black problems. Today, many Americans believe that with the passage of the Civil Rights Act and the implementation of affirmative action programs, blacks have been given more than a fair chance to succeed. In fact, many whites feel that liberals and Democrats have fulfilled the demands of black Americans at the expense of whites. The recent Republican administrations have succeeded in manipulating and dominating the "politics of race," repeatedly blaming immigrants or minorities for societal problems. Anti-Asian sentiment and violence also have increased. Furthermore, some scholars argue that the neoconservative policies of the Republican administrations have pitted minority groups against one another, in the form of Korean–African American and Latino–African American tensions, which led to the rise of antiminority violence during the 1980s. It is consistent with the historical development of majority-minority relations that the power structure should blame the victims for social problems in this country.

Police Brutality and the Justice System

Police brutality has long been a major problem for African Americans living in the inner city, and African American communities have long complained that it was common for black suspects to be harassed and insulted by Los Angeles Police Department (LAPD) officers. Police officers often stop young black men just because they are in the wrong neighborhood or are driving a car deemed beyond their legitimate means. Indeed, the Watts riots were triggered by the mistreatment of an African American suspect by a California Highway Patrol officer. Although the videotape of the beating of Rodney King shocked and outraged most Americans, for African Americans, it was nothing more than confirmation of their daily reality.

This distrust and enmity between the police and African American and Latino youths contributed to the explosion of the city in 1992. An aide to an elected black official commented that

the black community is under siege from the fall-out of racism, gangs, drugs and violence. If I am walking down the street and see some gangbangers on the one side and LAPD car on the other, I am not really sure which group I'm more afraid of. But actually, I feel more threatened by the police. (Glazer 1975a, p. 15)

Independent investigations of the Los Angeles Police Department confirmed major problems in the LAPD's treatment of minority communities (Tucker Committee 1992, p. 11). Therefore, the Christopher Commission (1991), the Webster Commission (1992), and the Tucker Committee (1992) all recommended systematic changes in the LAPD to establish a positive relationship with Los Angeles's diverse communities.

Before the Rodney King trial verdicts, city officials and community leaders warned of the possibility of widespread violence in the city, and Police Chief Daryl Gates publicly declared that he had set aside $1 million to pay for overtime in putting down any civil unrest. Yet the Webster Commission's report found that Gates and the LAPD had no such plan (Special Advisor 1992, p. 18). In fact, the report called it "the across-the-board failure in the planning function at every level of the emergency response to the civil disorder that erupted on April 29, 1992" (p. 85) When the violence erupted, Chief Gates left his post to attend a political fundraiser to defeat the Christopher Commission's reform initiative. Moreover, Gates never declared a tactical alert to put down the violence. As State Senator Diane Watson asserted, "Daryl Gates was in a position to allow the black community to go up in flames. And he did!" (Institute for Alternative Journalism 1992, p. 43).

Summary

The social, economic, and political conditions of south central Los Angeles and the ideological shifts to the right were the principal causes of the 1992 Los Angeles riots. In the 1960s, many African Americans had been optimistic that they could improve their lives by gaining political power and equal rights. Nevertheless, despite the warning of the Kerner Commission's report, the conditions of south central Los Angeles and African American communities in the United States continued to deteriorate during the 1980s and the early 1990s. Now, in the late 1990s, despair, hopelessness, and a sense of abandonment are widespread in African American communities.

2

A New Urban Crisis
Korean–African American Relations

The seeds of tension between Korean Americans and African Americans were sown and nourished during the 1970s and 1980s. While the African American community was stagnating economically, the Korean American community was thriving. And while the African American community watched capital flow out of the central city, the Korean American community put to work its internally generated capital.

Korean immigrant entrepreneurs found business opportunities in black neighborhoods as early as the late 1960s and early 1970s and established an economic niche by opening "wig stores" in the spaces vacated by stores abandoned or destroyed during the race riots of 1960s. These merchants found that the price of buying a small business in an African American neighborhood was lower than it was in white areas and that black customers seemed less concerned about the price of products than suburban customers were. One small-business owner we interviewed recalled advice he received when he first arrived in America: "I was told to open a small business in an African American area if I wanted to make lots of money in a short period of time." Thus, many Korean immigrants assumed that they could make a healthy profit from only a small investment of capital, and they did not intend to stay in African American neighborhoods for a long time. Of course, they did not anticipate the heavy price they would pay during the civil unrest of 1992 and the many boycotts of Korean-owned stores in several American cities during the 1980s and 1990s.

The relations between Korean Americans and African Americans in Los Angeles mirror relations between the two communities in other cities in the United States, notably Philadelphia (Jo 1992, Yu 1980) and New York (Cheng and Espiritu 1989, Min 1996, Park 1997, Yoon 1997). In all these other cities, the tensions between the communities have, from the

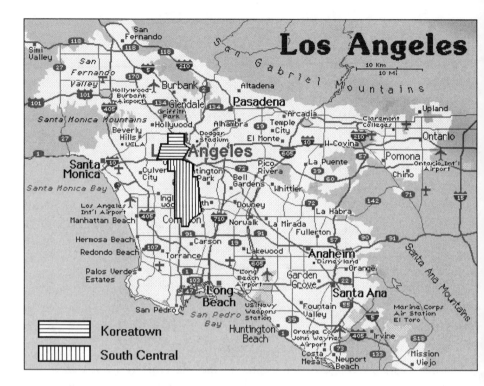

beginning, revolved around the "merchant" role of the Korean American community and the "customer" role of the African American community (Chang 1990, Light and Bonacich 1988, Yu 1990). Blacks boycott Korean stores, complaining of the Korean store owners' rudeness, and Koreans criticize African American customers' rudeness and dishonesty (Hutchinson 1991). These feelings came to a head when Korean American businesses were targeted by blacks during the 1992 Los Angeles riots.

The unease between customers and merchants was intensified by difficulties in communication, differences in culture, and the limited opportunities available for Korean Americans and African Americans to interact with each other except as merchant and customer. African American protesters often labeled Korean immigrant merchants as "aliens" who had "taken over" their community. For example, in New York City, one resident who was part of an angry group of protesters wore a button that declared "At War." The demonstrators distributed fliers urging African Americans to "boycott all Korean merchants," whom they accused of siphoning dollars from New York's West 125th Street community (*New*

York Times, January 19, 1985; *Korea Times,* January 22, 1985).[1] These many conflicts, protests, and boycotts eventually led to the highly publicized boycott of two Korean stores in Brooklyn, New York, between January 1990 and May 1991 (we will discuss this case in more detail later).

With the proliferation of Korean-owned businesses in south central Los Angeles, several of the stores have become the target of resentment, hostility, bigotry, boycotts, and sometimes violence by African Americans. In an open letter (April 7, 1985), the Concerned African American Citizens of Crenshaw/Western/Inglewood accused Korean businesses of "raping the African American community as they have done in Harlem." The *Los Angeles Sentinel* (a weekly African American newspaper) expressed concern in an editorial (June 20, 1985) that "in recent years, in the African American community, there has been what seems like an invasion of the Third World people. In many cases, they have become merchants in stores in our communities that were once owned by Whites, and later sold to members of other ethnic groups."

One of the first signs of potential conflict between the African American and Korean American communities was the publication of a series of negative editorials by the *Los Angeles Sentinel* in August and September 1983. According to James Cleaver, the paper's executive editor, the problem is not simply academic and philosophical: "African American folks are angry because here are a bunch of foreigners, a bunch of folks who don't speak English, who can't vote, who come here with money, and that is how it is perceived" (*Los Angeles Times,* June 8, 1984). Cleaver noted that the "African American community has literally been taken over by Asians in the past five years" (*Los Angeles Sentinel,* August 11, 1983), and he urged fellow African Americans to boycott Korean-owned stores.[2]

A few months later, a highly inflammatory article intensified the conflict between the two communities in Los Angeles. B. W. Swain, the publisher of *Money Talks News* (March 15–31, 1984), in a front-page story entitled "The Flight of African American Dollars $$$$$$$," urged community residents "not to give a dime to Koreans." He complained that Koreans were reluctant to hire African Americans and were hard to communicate with.[3] During the one-day boycott (November 18, 1989) of the Slauson Indoor Swap Meet, protesters carried signs asking, "How many times have you been mistreated and disrespected?" "How many African-Americans are working in Korean-owned businesses?"

The worsening relations between African Americans and Korean Americans were first publicly acknowledged in 1983 when the Los Angeles

Human Relations Commission convened a hearing to discuss difficulties in community relations resulting from allegations that Korean merchants were rude to their black customers (Chang 1992). As a result of these hearings, the Human Relations Commission helped develop the Black-Korean Alliance, a group of representatives from community and business organizations whose purpose was to facilitate communication and understanding between the communities.

In April 1986, four Korean merchants were killed by African Americans during robbery attempts (Chang 1992). Although these murders had no specific racial motivation, they nevertheless were a sign of the mounting conflict between the two communities. Between 1986 and 1991, community relations on the whole continued to be hostile, despite some positive interactions between Korean merchants and African American customers. For example, the Black-Korean Alliance sponsored numerous activities that brought together Koreans and African Americans in church and cultural functions, as well as in positive business enterprises. But the communities largely remained separated by their cultural and economic differences.

In 1991, these differences boiled over when on May 16, Latasha Harlins, a young black girl, was shot to death by Soon Ja Du, a Korean store owner. Although Mrs. Du was found guilty of manslaughter, she was sentenced to only five years' probation with no jail term, a sentence that outraged the African American community. Although the verdict was sharply criticized by the *Korea Times* as a travesty of justice, the Du case ignited the African American community's remnant feelings of injustice at the hands of the criminal court system. In response to the verdict, the Brotherhood Crusade, an African American organization with strong community ties, developed an economic and social plan whose cornerstone was the eventual removal of Korean-owned stores from black neighborhoods (Mitchell 1991). Then in June 1991, three months after Latasha Harlins was killed, Lee Arthur Mitchell was shot by Tae Sam Park, a Korean merchant. This latest tragedy brought out the African American community's anger, frustration, and resentment toward the police, politicians, media, poverty, and Korean American merchants. Although the police investigation ruled this a "justifiable homicide," African American groups chose to boycott the Korean store, charging that the Los Angeles Police Department's ruling of "justifiable homicide" was premature. Protesters demanded that the district attorney's office indict and prosecute Mr. Park for the murder.

Less than a year later, the April 1992 riots broke out. Although they were a truly multicultural response to economic, political, and social conditions in Los Angeles (Davis 1992, Omi and Winant 1993), the tension between African Americans and Korean Americans was paramount (Kim 1993). In the melee, 2,073 Korean-owned stores were burned down, with nearly 50 percent of the total damage in Los Angeles (Ong and Hee 1993). The disproportionate level of destruction experienced by the Korean community led to the belief that Korean stores had been targeted, a belief that was eventually corroborated by an FBI investigation (Hwangbo 1992).

A Sociological Analysis of Korean American and African American Relations

The Los Angeles riots of 1992 and the highly publicized boycotts of Korean-owned stores by African American residents in Los Angeles and New York have forced scholars and observers to pay closer attention to conflicts between minority groups, and scholars (Abelmann and Lie 1995, Bonacich and Jung 1982, Chang 1990, Freer 1994, H. Lee 1993, Min 1996, Park 1997, Yoon 1997) have offered a number of theories to explain them. The relations between the two communities can be described using the theory of "middleman minorities" (Bonacich 1973, Min 1996). As a middleman minority, Korean Americans are in the middle in terms of not only economic relations but also social relations arising from their economic status. They thus are the recipients of hostility from both the dominant culture and the subordinate group. The dominant culture's hostility is aimed at middleman groups when a foreign group (in this case, Koreans) enters already occupied economic niches, thereby eliciting the antagonism of different business elements in the host society's dominant culture (Bonacich 1973). In Los Angeles's Korean American community, this antagonism has ranged from responses by city hall to complaints regarding traffic congestion and parking in the Koreatown area, to the repeal of free trade laws in the liquor industry and the subsequent increase in competition between chain-owned and family-owned liquor stores, to short-term changes in the Small Business Administration's loan policies that have hampered the Korean American community's ability to obtain external sources of funding (Light and Bonacich 1988). These measures, though arguably not intended as a direct response to the

Korean American community, nevertheless have reined in Korean economic expansion.

The Korean community's response to such perceived hostility has usually been to strengthen the ethnic enclave by developing ethnically based organizations such as the Korean American Grocery Association (Light and Bonacich 1988, Min 1996). These organizations serve the dual function of securing Korean economic interests while reinforcing the community's internal solidarity. Not surprisingly, Min (1996) described the Korean immigrant merchant as "caught in the middle" in America's multiethnic cities.

Hostility between middlemen and the customers they serve has a more immediate effect than does tension between middlemen and the host society. Since customers and merchants interact with one another on a daily basis, their relations are based on these day-to-day interactions and the perceptions of the middlemen's economic role in the community. According to Light and Bonacich (1988), African Americans have accused Korean store owners of not investing their profits back into the communities in which they do business and of consistently hiring Koreans instead of blacks. In addition, African Americans feel that Koreans treat them rudely, a belief that has only increased the resentment of many blacks toward Koreans' business success.

According to the middleman minority theory, there are two reasons for the antagonism between the two communities: (1) Korean American merchants take resources from the African American community, which are eventually either consumed by Korean Americans or passed on to the dominant culture; and (2) Korean Americans serve as "scapegoats" by absorbing the anger usually directed at the dominant group (primarily white). This latter point refers to the fact that one reason the black community has been unable to achieve the economic success of many Korean Americans is their history of economic discrimination (see Bunch 1992, Case 1972, Davis 1992, de Graaf 1970, Norman 1992).

Although the middleman minority theory may be useful for understanding economic intergroup conflict, it cannot be applied uniformly without qualifications. In Los Angeles, only 10 percent of Korean-owned businesses are located in areas with a predominantly African American clientele (Yu 1990). According to the Korean American Grocers Association's (KAGRO) 1994 survey of 461 Korean American merchants in Los Angeles, 17.4 percent of Korean American stores cater primarily to African American customers (table 2.1), and nearly half (48 percent) of

TABLE 2.1
Customer Base (%) of Korean-Owned Businesses

	Los Angeles		Dallas[b]	New York[b]
African Americans	10[a]	17.4[b]	34	39
Asian Americans	22		5	3
Latinos	17	53.2	40	37
Whites	48	25.6	21	19

SOURCES: [a]Eui-Young Yu, *Korean Community Profile: Life and Consumer Patterns* (Los Angeles: *Korea Times*, 1990), p. 10. [b]*National Korean American Grocer (NKA-GRO) Journal* 3 (July-August 1994): 32-33.

Korean-owned businesses in Southern California are located in areas that serve mainly whites.

In the wake of the 1992 riots, Korean immigrant merchants are moving out of south central Los Angeles, and the traditional mom-and-pop stores (liquor and grocery stores, dry cleaners, and gas stations) are being replaced by wholesale and franchise businesses. According to the *Los Angeles Times* (November 5, 1997), Korean Americans for the first time are showing a collective interest in franchises. For example, because of grueling hours, constant disputes with customers, and the 1992 Los Angeles riots that left his business in ruins, Matt Kim decided to leave the dry cleaning establishment in south central Los Angeles that he had operated for fifteen years. Therefore, labeling Korean immigrant merchants only as "middleman minority" is an inaccurate description of the economic reality of the Korean immigrant community in Los Angeles after the 1992 civil unrest. Furthermore, many Korean-owned businesses sell products produced in and imported from Asian countries, such as South Korea, Taiwan, Hong Kong, Singapore, and China (Chang 1990, Yoon 1997).

The resentment of African Americans toward Korean Americans has been heightened by the growing distance between the communities. As Koreans strengthened their community internally in order to face the challenges presented by the host society, they further solidified the cultural wall between themselves and the African American community. As discussed by Bonacich and Modell (1980), the functional role of the middleman minority in the host society has served to create a closed circle of antagonism. From a sociological perspective, the conflict between African Americans and Korean Americans is a manifestation of their roles in the larger socioeconomic framework, with ethnicity simply the dimension along which tensions arise (Azar and Burton 1986). Beneath these visible signs of tension lie psychological dynamics that also, to some degree, emanate from the relationship between the communities.

Relations as Perceived by African Americans and Korean Americans

The continuing tensions between the Korean American and African American communities cannot be attributed solely to structural conditions. Rather, a social interaction initiated by one party generates a response from the other that in turn generates a return response (Pruitt and Rubin 1986). Thus the role of perceptions and attitudes is particularly important to interethnic relations, since conflict between ethnic groups can be conceptualized as developing in the "border zones" where the two cultures meet, intermingle, and sometimes clash (Tierney 1993). It is in these border zones that people begin to negotiate their different perceptions of reality. To understand the dialogue in this border zone and to connect it to community-based interventions, we conducted a survey of African American and Korean American perceptions of intergroup relations, between three and nine months after the civil unrest of April 1992. Our sample consisted of 178 Korean Americans and 165 African Americans. The Korean American sample ranged in age from twenty-one to sixty, with annual incomes of $0.00 to $200,000. Fifty-five percent of the sample were first-generation immigrants, and 45 percent were "one and a half" generation immigrants. Forty-six percent of the sample were female and 43 percent were male. The African American sample ranged in age from eighteen to sixty-nine, with annual incomes of $0.00 to $150,000. Thirty-seven percent of the sample were female and 59 percent were male. The respondents answered questions about their understanding of Korean American business success, tensions between their two communities, and what might be done to improve relations.

Reasons for Tensions between the African American and Korean American Communities

The principal categories of the two samples and percentages based on the total number of responses given are presented in table 2.2. Because a re-

TABLE 2.2
*Reasons for Tensions between African Americans
and Korean Americans*

Rank	Items	%
African American Respondents		
1	Communication and Culture	25
2	Korean Attitudes	24
3	Customer-Merchant Relations	20
4	Exploitation and Discrimination	13
5	Latasha Harlins's Murder	10
Korean American Respondents		
1	Communication and Culture	42
2	Korean Attitudes	15
3	African American Attitudes	14
4	General Economic and Social Structure	13
5	Mutual Prejudice and Racism	1

spondent could provide more than one reason and because not all persons answered the questions, the total number of responses does not always equal the number of respondents and differs across samples and across questions.

The five categories for the African American data are presented in descending order, with the first category being the one that received the most responses. The first category, "Communication and Culture," includes issues such as language barriers, differences in culture, a lack of understanding or knowledge of the other's history, and differences in nonverbal style and norms. Responses in this category covers statements like "Miscommunication and different cultural backgrounds; Korean business men and women often appear abrupt and abusive in their customer relations."

The second category, "Korean Attitudes," includes statement referring to Koreans' general attitudes and Korean American merchants' specific attitudes toward African Americans (e.g., prejudice, racism, disparagement of African Americans). Examples of responses in this category are "Koreans think they're better people. They treat all people like thieves unless they know you well"; "They are already programmed when they came to this country not to trust the blacks. But they make money from the people who live in the ghetto."

The third category, "Customer-Merchant Relations," refers to the behavior of Korean American merchants toward their customers (e.g., their following African American customers around the store) or to blacks' beliefs regarding the economic practices of Korean merchants (e.g., they don't put money back into the African American community). Examples are "They don't treat us with respect. I think we should be treated with respect when we're in their store"; "Koreans have a bad habit of wanting to shout at and disrespect blacks when they are being patronized by these same people."

The fourth category, "Exploitation and Discrimination," encompasses all those responses concerning structural and institutional discrimination against African Americans or the structural and institutional preferences of Korean Americans. For example, "When it comes to treatment on the political scale, you'll find that other races are given more chances in the business market"; "They don't give African Americans the same choice they give Koreans in order to better their condition."

The fifth category, "Latasha Harlins's Murder," covers all those items referring to either the shooting of Latasha Harlins or the sentence given to Mrs. Soon Ja Du. One African American respondent stated, "I feel that the main reasons for tensions between the African American and Korean communities is the incident that happened with Latasha Harlins."

In the Korean American sample, the first two categories were the same as those in the African American sample ("Communication and Culture" and "Korean Attitudes"). Some of the Korean American responses to "Culture and Communication" were "Lack of knowledge and understanding of each other. Lack of cultural commonplace [i.e., cultural similarity]." "Way of understanding. Way of thinking." The "Korean Attitudes" category elicited the following: "The Korean community is too centralized. We aren't as open-minded to other races as we should be"; "Korean Americans tend to be closed minded about other cultural history and look down on the black community."

The third category, "African American Attitudes," encompassed issues like African Americans' scapegoating Korean Americans or the prejudice of African Americans against Koreans. One Korean American respondent stated, "Redirected behavior—taking out their frustrations and blaming a group of people that make easier victims for their social problems that are based on their own failures from their inappropriate rationale and actions most of which culminated from the white oppressive societal history from which many had not choice from coming from."

The fourth category, "General Economic and Social Structure," included issues pertaining to both communities. For example, "I think the structure of the society is built wrong"; "poverty and social economic depression in the black community."

The final category, "Mutual Prejudice and Racism," referred to the attitudes of the two groups, for example, "I think that both communities have misperceptions of each other. Korean Americans perceive that African Americans are lazy and live on welfare, and African Americans think Koreans are rude and concerned only about money"; "misunderstanding, distrust, and prejudice by both African Americans and Koreans about the other group."

The similarity between the two communities is apparent. For both groups, the most important reasons for tensions concern cultural differences (e.g., language barriers, a lack of understanding of each other's culture), although a much larger percentage of the Korean respondents believed this than did the African Americans. Both communities placed a roughly equal emphasis on Korean attitudes as a reason for the tension, although a larger percentage of African Americans stressed this aspect than did the Korean Americans. But whereas the Korean sample did place relatively larger emphasis on African American attitudes, for the African American respondents, this category was not one of the largest, with only about 5 percent of African American respondents stating that their own attitudes were an important reason for tensions between the two groups.

Several of the differences between the two samples were substantial. For example, whereas 20 percent of African Americans indicated that customer-merchant relations contributed to the tension, this category did not even register in the Korean American sample. Similarly, 10 percent of African American respondents indicated that the murder of Latasha Harlins and the relatively light sentence given to Mrs. Du were important reasons for the unease, but none of the Korean sample cited this as a reason for the tension between the two communities.

Whereas both communities listed economic issues as a reason for tensions, the Korean sample referred to the impoverished economic and social climate of many of their inner-city neighbors, as well as the economic disparities between the two communities. The African American sample, in contrast, talked about general issues of historical exploitation and discrimination as well as specific issues related to Korean economic behavior (e.g., their not putting money back into the African American community and taking over the African American community).

Resolving the Tensions

Table 2.3 lists the responses to the question, "How would you suggest that tensions between the communities be resolved?" The breakdown of responses within each category is by percentages, which were calculated in the same way as for table 2.2.

In the African American sample in table 2.3, the largest category, "Building Coalitions and Communication," included suggestions for building coalitions, cross-community partnerships, and various intergroup working relationships. For example, "Knowledge of each other's culture; sharing and working together more to attain similar goals"; and "I feel that the tensions between the communities [can] be resolved if both parties would be willing to compromise, work together, and help each other out."

The second category, "Treat African Americans with Respect and Equity," elicited statements such as "Maybe if they [Koreans] would let you decide on what you want to do first, look around, and then let you ask them for assistance. No, as soon as you walk through the door they [Koreans] are right behind you"; and "The African American should receive the same treatment every other racial group does, and this will reduce or, better yet, help remove tensions over time."

The third category, "Improve African American Economic Opportunities," brought suggestions like "Get a substantial amount of black-owned business for Africans to go to"; or "Employ blacks to do more than sitting and watching other blacks to make sure they're not stealing."

The fourth category, "Change Korean Economic Behavior," listed statements such as "Employment of African Americans in Korean stores in our community. Limit the number of liquor stores in the community and put money back into the community." The final category, "Separate Communities/Not Possible," was for those responses indicating either that it was simply not possible to improve relations or that the only way to decrease tensions was to remove Korean American stores from African American neighborhoods and/or stop interactions altogether between the two communities. For example, "Give the Afro American man or woman respect first, and then separate the communities"; "I don't think it will ever be resolved."

For the Korean data, the largest category was "Build coalitions and understanding." One Korean respondent thought that "with communi-

TABLE 2.3
*How Tensions between African Americans and
Korean Americans Can Be Solved*

Rank	Items	%
African American Respondents		
1	Build coalitions and understanding	56
2	Treat African Americans with respect and equality	16
3	Improve African Americans' economic opportunities	12
4	Change Koreans' economic behavior	7
5	Separate communities/Not possible	10
Korean American Respondents		
1	Build coalitions and understanding	68
2	Change Koreans' attitude and behavior	16
3	Change economic and social structure	9
4	Change biased media coverage	7

cation and collaboration, it is possible to untangle the problem." Another suggested that "various exchange programs, for example, cultural exchange programs, should be developed to get to know each other and to understand that they share more than they can imagine as victims of the white-dominant society." The second category, "Change Korean Attitudes and Behavior," referred to the need for the Korean American community to become more open-minded and to change their behavior toward African Americans to reflect a more understanding attitude. For example, "I think we K-As should understand the black culture and be open-minded and communicate with them to solve difficult problems."

Responses to the third category, "Change Economic and Social Structure," pertained to modifying the United States's social infrastructure. One Korean American stated, "To battle chronic and widespread social and economic problems in the African American community, Koreans and African Americans must demand and achieve social and economic reforms from the government."

The final category, "Change Biased Media Coverage," contained statements like "The mass media and community leaders need to stop thinking that there is racial struggle. The mass media's portrayal of both groups ignite hatred toward each other"; and "lobbying to stop distorted media coverage regarding the tension."

By far the largest category in both communities concerned issues related to building coalitions and improving understanding between two communities. Fifty-six percent of the African American responses fell into this category, as did 66 percent of the Korean American responses. The second largest category in both samples had to do with changing Korean American attitudes toward African Americans. For both samples, the third largest category had to do with changing the groups' economic and social behavior, although the way in which people characterized it differed for each sample. For African Americans, these changes were related specifically to improving the economic opportunities for African Americans, whereas in the Korean American sample, these changes pertained more broadly to changing the general structure of society.

Understanding Korean Americans' Business Success

Korean Americans and African Americans have different opinions about why Korean Americans are more successful at running businesses than African Americans are. The majority of Korean Americans (70 percent) believe that their strict work ethic and frugality have helped them establish businesses in America. In response, African American leaders charge that the lack of black capitalism is due to institutionalized discrimination and racism (Marable 1983). Many African American–owned businesses fail because they are undercapitalized and the owners and/or workers lack the relevant skills and thus are unable to compete with well-financed white corporations. Our survey found that 71 percent of African Americans believe discrimination by financial institutions keeps them from obtaining loans to open small businesses.

More important, the majority of African American respondents believed that Korean Americans receive special help from financial institutions and government agencies that enable their small businesses to succeed (table 2.4)—even though Korean Americans do not receive any special loans or assistance from government agencies or financial institutions. In fact, recent Korean immigrants are often refused loans from financial institutions because of government red tape, their insufficient U.S. credit history, and their lack of information about Small Business Administration loans. Instead, many Korean immigrants rely on *kyes* (rotating credit associations) to accumulate capital and finance their business.

TABLE 2.4

Why Korean Americans Are More Successful at Opening
Businesses Than African Americans

	African Americans (%)	Korean Americans (%)
Koreans are willing to work longer hours than are African Americans.	44	70
Koreans are better at saving money than are African Americans.	36	57
Koreans receive stronger economic support from their community than do African Americans.	76	34
African Americans don't support African American–owned businesses.	58	10
Koreans get special treatment by non-Korean-owned banks.	54	7
Los Angeles politicians help Koreans get established more than they help African Americans.	60	0.05
Because of discrimination it's difficult for African Americans to get loans to open small businesses.	71	34

Stereotypes and Prejudice

Our survey of 121 Korean Americans confirms that their attitudes toward African Americans are negative. The majority believed that African Americans should try harder to become self-sufficient by obtaining a good education and developing strong family values (table 2.5). In addition, just over one-third (34 percent) of the respondents expressed concern for their safety by agreeing with the statement that "Koreans should always watch out for safety when they are with African Americans." Not all Korean American perceptions of African Americans are negative, however: 60 percent of the respondents indicated that African Americans had many positive qualities to contribute to Los Angeles.

According to our survey, African Americans do not have a favorable view of Korean American merchants (table 2.6), as 74 percent answered that "Koreans care more about profits than about people." Furthermore, 65 percent complained about the rudeness of Korean merchants, and almost half (53 percent) of the respondents indicated that they didn't trust Korean merchants because they believed that they charged higher prices than did the owners of other small businesses.

According to Byran Jackson's survey of African Americans in Los Angeles, Asians are the least-liked ethnic group. Conducted in June 1988,

TABLE 2.5
Korean Americans' Perception of African Americans

African Americans on welfare could get along without it if they tried.	62%
African Americans place a low value on family and education.	60
African Americans have many positive things to contribute to Los Angeles.	60
Koreans should always watch out for their safety when they are with African Americans.	34

TABLE 2.6
African Americans' Perception of Korean Merchants

Koreans do not treat African Americans with respect.	65%
Koreans care more about profits than people.	74
Koreans charge more for their goods than do owners of other small businesses.	53

TABLE 2.7
African Americans' Feelings about a Racial Group

	Close (%)	Not Close (%)
White	84.7	13.1
Jewish	69.9	25.1
Asian	62.4	32.7
Hispanic	83.7	14.8

African Americans' Feelings about Asians

	Close (%)	Not Close (%)
South central Los Angeles	65.7	32.7
Inglewood	61.1	38.9
Other areas	68.8	31.2
All Los Angeles	62.8	32.7

SOURCE: Byron O. Jackson, "The Consciousness and Political Behavior Survey," conducted in June 1988.

the survey was part of the research project "Los Angeles Racial Group Consciousness and Political Behavior Survey." By cross-tabulating Jackson's data, we were able to analyze African American attitudes toward different ethnic groups in three different geographical areas: south central Los Angeles, Inglewood, and other areas. As table 2.7 shows, African Americans in Los Angeles feel closer to whites, Hispanics, and Jews than to Asians. Almost one-third (32.7 percent) percent of the African American respondents had negative feelings about Asians, a much higher percentage than that for whites (13.1 percent), Jews (25.1 percent), and Hispanics (14.8 percent).

Interestingly, the Jackson survey found that the residents of the middle-class community of Inglewood had more negative attitudes toward Asians (38.9 percent) than did the residents of south central Los Angeles (34.3 percent). Although this is a difference of only 4.6 percent, it still is significant because many residents of Inglewood usually do not have daily contact with Korean American merchants. This finding suggests that African Americans' negative attitudes toward Asians (particularly Korean Americans) do not necessarily arise from direct contact with them (e.g., between customers and merchants).

Prospects for Intergroup Cooperation

What is the prospect for creating cooperative relations between the Korean American and African American communities? Can they overcome communication, cultural, and language barriers and find a common ground? As we can see from table 2.8, both Korean Americans and African Americans were generally receptive to the idea of intergroup cooperation. In particular, Korean Americans (68 percent) and African Americans (70 percent) were willing to cooperate in creating jobs for African Americans. Both groups (52 percent of African Americans and 78 percent of Korean Americans) felt that they needed to work harder to get to know each other better. In addition, 75 percent of African Americans and 59 percent of Korean Americans stated that they were willing to work together to rebuild Los Angeles. However, only 20 percent of African

TABLE 2.8
Ways for Koreans and African Americans to Work Together

	African Americans (%)	Korean Americans (%)
Attend each other's churches and community events	20	64
Work together to rebuild Los Angeles	75	59
Cooperate in developing jobs for African Americans	70	68
Get to know each other	52	78
Open Korean-owned banks in African American neighborhoods	14	6
Support each other's stores	17	15

Americans were willing to participate in and attend Korean American community events and churches, whereas 60 percent of Korean Americans were willing to do likewise. A small percentage of Korean Americans (15 percent) and African Americans (17 percent) were willing to support each other's stores, and an even smaller percentage of African Americans (14 percent) and Korean Americans (6 percent) endorsed the idea of opening Korean-owned banks in African American neighborhoods. These findings suggest that economic cooperation between Korean Americans and African Americans seems to be the best way to establish a cooperative relationship between the two communities.

Confrontation: Racial or Economic?

Even while tensions between Korean merchants and black customers escalate, members of the African American community repeatedly deny that race is the principal factor. When four Korean merchants were shot and killed in April 1986, some people feared that it was a racially motivated crime. South central Los Angeles and other inner-city neighborhoods do have high crime rates, but crime, drugs, and violence affect African American residents more than they do Korean merchants. And more often than not, African American residents are the victims of African American crimes. For example, in Los Angeles, African Americans were victims of 45.1 percent of the homicides in 1987, whereas Asians accounted for only 2.2 percent.

Koreans have to bear the burden of crime because their businesses are located in high-risk neighborhoods, and racial and ethnic differences may add to the risk. But even if some African American assailants have a special hatred for Korean merchants, it is almost impossible to know whether it is the motive for their crimes. "Many of the robbery or murder cases are accidental rather than planned by criminals," noted one observer. "I don't think that American assailants target Koreans because they dislike or hate 'Koreans.'" Along with safety, Korean businessmen are concerned about organized boycotts of their stores, activities that are perceived as anti-Korean because they directly challenge the livelihood of Korean immigrants.

Theories of Interethnic Conflict

Culture as a Source of Difference

The clash of cultures between Korean immigrant merchants and African American customers is often cited as a possible source of conflict. African American customers complain that Korean merchants treat them with disrespect and that the merchants cannot communicate with them. "Monocultural people [i.e., Koreans] doing business in a multi-cultural society is potentially problematic. Particularly, south central Los Angeles is probably the worst place Koreans can come into," declared Larry Aubry of Los Angeles County Human Relations Commission, adding that "Koreans don't know how to interact with customers."[4] And as Melanie Lomax, vice president of the NAACP, observed, "It is clear these [Korean immigrants] are hard-working and industrious. But there's a high degree of resentment being bred against them in the African American community." Lomax claims that cultural differences account for most of the disputes between Korean merchants and African American customers. "We've identified it as cultural differences—both groups are not particularly educated about the other's cultural heritage" (*Los Angeles Times*, April 15, 1985).

Stewart found that Koreans and African Americans have different sets of rules concerning proper attitudes and behaviors and that violations of these rules elicit negative reactions. "Korean merchants most frequently mentioned loudness, bad language, and shoplifting as inappropriate behaviors by black patrons, stating that African American patrons should have shown respect and courtesy, and should have apologized more frequently." African American patrons most frequently mentioned Korean merchants' or employees' negative attitude—being ignored and being watched constantly, as well as having money thrown on the counter—as inappropriate behaviors (Stewart 1989, chap. 2, p. 2).

The media also tend to emphasize cultural differences and misunderstandings as the main source of conflict between Korean merchants and African American customers. In fact, communication is a problem, owing not only to the language barrier but also to each group's different expectations of social interactions. For example, Korean merchants are not likely to make direct eye contact with any of their customers, regardless of their race, because they have been taught to not make eye contact with older people and strangers. Such a gesture is considered not only rude and disrespectful but also a direct challenge to the other person's authority. Unfortunately, African American customers often interpret such behavior as a sign of the merchant's disrespect. At the same time, Korean merchants also complain about the "bad language" and loudness of their African American customers, behavior they regard as a sign of aggressiveness and also disrespect. Clearly, cultural differences can create misunderstandings and bad feelings, fueling and intensifying racial and ethnic conflict.

The Economic Causes of Conflict

Cultural differences are not the only cause of the tension between African Americans and Korean Americans. For instance, many Korean immigrant merchants have no historical understanding or awareness of the American civil rights movement and U.S. race relations in general. Rather, the content or quality of interaction between Korean merchants and African American residents is more likely either to minimize or escalate tension.

The underrepresentation of African American businesses in the United States has also been cited as a possible source of resentment. Historically, non–African American merchants have dominated the economy of African American communities in the United States, even though many African American leaders have recommended self-help, or economic development, as a way to improve their communities. One of the earliest advocates of self-help was Booker T. Washington, who believed that blacks should get a good education and learn new skills to prove their worthiness to white America. But Washington's views were severely criticized by other African American leaders because he accepted the principles of the "separate but equal" doctrine. In a similar vein, Marcus Garvey, the leader of the Universal Negro Improvement Association (UNIA), urged African Americans to learn industrial and vocational skills, but he was discredited when the federal government indicted him in connection with the sale of stock in his African American Star Line. Today, however, the Urban League, the National Association for Advancement of Colored People (NAACP), and other African American organizations are actively pushing for African American economic development. But despite attempts to improve the black community's economic conditions, the number of African American–owned businesses has remained relatively small.

Several scholars (Hurh and Kim 1984, Kim 1981, Light and Bonacich 1988, Min 1988) have theorized that Koreans' ethnic solidarity and middle-class backgrounds ("ethclass" resources) have facilitated the proliferation of Korean ethnic entrepreneurship in America. Light (1972) dismissed the "ethnic consumer market" theory and proposed the lack of ethnic cohesiveness as the main cause of the lack of African American–owned businesses in America. Light argued that despite racism and discrimination, Asian Americans were able to establish small businesses by forming "rotating credit associations," based on "ascriptive" characteristics. African American businesses failed, however, because of the lack of ethnic cohesiveness based on blood and land. Coles named white racism as the main obstacle to African American economic development because it affected every aspect of their life. He suggested that African Americans have created compensatory consumption patterns because "they have been deprived of much of this world's material goods, and the acquisition of such items as TV, automobiles, and sundry household appliances becomes a major achievement" (1975, pp. 49, 59).

Being totally ignored by a merchant is an especially sensitive issue for many African American patrons. "I patronize the gas station because a Korean lady always greets me with 'hello' and never forgets to say have a nice day," said one man. "Across from that gas station, there is an African American–owned gas station. But he has never said hello or been friendly to me. Thus, I patronize the Korean-owned gas station." An African American resident remarked that "the Koreans obviously lack respect for African Americans as a whole." Protesters at a Korean store held picket signs stating, "Cultural Difference? A Smile Is Universal." "Your Pride Is More Valuable Than a Free Clock." "They Call Us 'Nigger' in There."

Stewart found that "being watched while shopping was the most frequently mentioned rule violation by African American patrons."[5] In fact, many African American customers objected to the Korean merchants' lack of respect. Stewart found that African Americans often complain that "they are always watching you. They treat you like a criminal or 'dirt' by watching you all the time. When I go in their stores, I know I am going to be watched so I go in with an attitude" (1989, chap. 3, p. 11).

Racial attitudes also are learned and reinforced through the media. Some scholars (Chang 1990, Jo 1992, Yoon 1997) proposed that Korean immigrants form their negative perceptions of African Americans before coming to the United States, whereas Min (1996) argued that Korean immigrants come to America without negative racial stereotypes of African

Americans but learn them soon after they arrive. In any case, the mass media's depiction of African Americans as uneducated, poor, or criminal influences Koreans' perceptions either before or after they immigrate. And because many Korean-owned stores are located in poor African American neighborhoods with high crime rates, these negative stereotypes are often reinforced by their personal experiences with African American customers.

African American residents often regard Korean merchants as "aliens," "foreigners," or "outsiders" who are "ripping them off" or exploiting the African American community. Under these circumstances, conflicts can be explosive and have long-lasting consequences for U.S. society as a whole. During the early 1980s, Asian (i.e., Korean) immigrants were conveniently blamed by American workers for the trade deficit and high unemployment rates. Economist Milton Friedman commented on the U.S. media's distortion of the trade deficit issue: "What struck me most forcefully was the near universal acceptance of the stereotypes that dominate media reporting of international trade issues."[6] Reflecting this growing anti-Asian (i.e., anti-Korean) sentiment, Los Angeles City Councilman Nate Holden introduced a proposal entitled "Stop Selling America," which would prohibit non-U.S. citizens from purchasing property in Los Angeles. Holden argued that "we are watching our precious land, a finite resource, being sold to foreigners to satisfy the greed of a few. . . . Our founding fathers never had intentions of selling our country to foreigners" (*Los Angeles Herald*, June 30, 1988).[7]

Unaware of the history of oppression and exploitation of minority groups by white America, many Korean immigrants have little sympathy for poor African Americans. Instead, their thinking is centered on their belief that America is a "land of opportunities." Korean immigrants often have no respect for African American customers who are unemployed and dependent on government programs, as they believe that African Americans should not blame anyone except themselves for their situation.

Black Nationalism

Mr. Kim, the owner of a women's clothing store, reacted angrily to an African American "boycott" of his store. "I can't afford to hire anyone. Also, we try to be friendly to the customers. We know that we have to be kind and friendly to the customers if we want to make more profits.

However, they curse at me many times. How can I smile at them while they curse at me?" Several scholars (H. Lee 1993, Min 1996, Yoon 1997) have noted that the resurgence of black nationalism was successful in organizing and mobilizing African American residents against Korean American merchants portrayed as "foreigners" or "outsiders" that exploited the African American community. Calling for economic self-sufficiency and political autonomy, the black nationalist ideology attacked Korean merchants as hampering the African American community's economic and political progress. In this way, blacks can rationalize their boycotts of Korean-owned stores.

African American and Jewish Relations as a Comparison

The conflict between African Americans and Korean Americans is certainly not the first interethnic conflict stemming from economic and structural relations. Blacks and Jews (another middleman minority group) also have a history of both intergroup conflict and cooperation.

There are many similarities between African Americans' complaints about Jewish merchants and also Korean immigrant merchants. Both Jewish and Korean merchants are accused of being "money chasers," of "overcharging for inferior products," and of "exploiting the African American community for their own enrichment." As these African American women complained about Jewish merchants: "They all cheat." "They have to cheat 'cause we don't have nowhere else to go" (Katz 1967, p. 76). In addition, Jewish merchants have been accused of being "outsiders" plotting to take over African American communities. "Koreans are buying buildings from Jewish owners which usually are run down buildings. Jewish owners can sell the building way above real value to Koreans, thus, African Americans have no chance of purchasing the buildings. . . . Koreans increase rent to African American tenants, thus, kicking them out" (*Korea Times*, May 30, 1984; *Metro News*, May 12, 1984).

The relationship of Jews and African Americans has been described as a "bitter-sweet encounter," because it has fluctuated between cooperation and conflict (Weisbord and Stein 1970). Some scholars have described Jews and blacks as natural allies because of Jews' strong support of the antislavery struggles of the nineteenth century and the civil rights movement of the 1960s (Glazer 1969, Marx 1967). Even so, anti-Semitism among African Americans rose during the 1960s. In his introductory remarks during the Jewish–African American symposium, Shlomo Katz

(1967) commented that (1) a pronounced anti-Jewish sentiment exists among African Americans in this country, and (2) Jews are reacting to this sentiment with an emotional backlash. Their relations have been further strained in recent years by anti-Semitic remarks by Jesse Jackson and Louis Farrakhan. In a related study of Los Angeles's African American community, Tsukashima stated that "African American anti-Semitism resulted from the perceived or real economic inequality between African Americans and Jews (especially those economic exchanges in which there has developed a collective perception on the part of a less powerful, poorer minority that another minority has tended to make undue profit out of it)" (1986, p. 12).

Jews and Korean Americans have been portrayed as "superachievers" and/or a "model minority," terms implying that Jews and Korean Americans have surpassed African Americans economically, even though most African Americans have been in the United States longer. Such labels frustrate African Americans, adding to their resentment for not being able to succeed. Accordingly, they use Jewish and Korean merchants as scapegoats for their own lack of economic and social advancement. Why can't African Americans achieve as much as Korean immigrants or Jews have, who have succeeded without government assistance? Simply put, African Americans are blamed for their failure, and African Americans criticize Jewish and Korean merchants for making a living by exploiting their African American customers. In *Notes of a Native Son*, James Baldwin observed, "Jews are identified with oppression and are hated for it. Jews own everything."[8] Katz explained African Americans' feelings about Jewish merchants:

> The poor African American's perception of a Jewish world is a very limited one: he knows little or nothing of Jewish culture, religion, or of the Jewish intellectual. African Americans do identify the Jews as the exploiting, cheating merchant who derives his income from ghetto dwellers, and takes it all out with him to his fancy home someplace else (Katz 1967, p. 76)

The relationship between Jews and African Americans and that between Koreans and African Americans are different in many respects. Whereas Korean immigrants are primarily owners of mom-and-pop stores in African American neighborhoods, Jewish–African American relations in the inner city extend beyond merchant-customer relations to landlord-tenant and teacher-student relations as well. In addition, the sociopolitical status of Korean Americans and Jewish Americans are quite different. Although Jewish Americans have faced prejudice, discrimination, and racism in America, they have succeeded in becoming part of the mainstream. Jews are an economically and politically powerful group in America. In contrast, most Korean Americans have been in the United States for less than twenty years, and they have not yet been able to attain political power. And whereas Korean Americans are seen as a favored minority, African Americans are critical of Jews whom they see as being part of a white America that dominates and controls every aspect of African American life. Baldwin asserted that "African Americans are anti-Semitic because they are anti-white" (1967, p. 27). Similarly, Bender noted that "Negroes reacted to Jews as white men, as perforce part of the white majority, even if they were perceived to be different within that majority" (Bender 1969, p. 64). Therefore, Jewish–African American relations may be regarded as more hierarchical and/or vertical, whereas Korean–African American relations are more horizontal. Since Korean and African Americans view themselves as equal or better than the other group, Korean–African American relations are potentially more explosive.

Despite these differences, the Jewish merchants of 1960s and the Korean merchants of 1990s suffered major damages during what have been characterized as "race riots." Thus far, we examined the historical circumstances that led to encounters between Korean immigrants and African Americans and Jewish merchants and African Americans. For many recent Korean immigrants, low-income African American neighborhoods provide the only location in which they can successfully manage a business with their limited proficiency in English and limited start-up capital.[9] Because economic survival is one of the most important issues facing Korean immigrants, some are willing to do anything to protect their economic interests.[10] The image of gun-toting Korean immigrants during the Los Angeles civil unrest of 1992 vividly reminds us how far some Korean merchants were willing to go to protect their property. This behavior was far different from that of many Jewish store owners who responded by leaving the south central area after the Watts riots in 1965. Many Americans wondered why the Korean store owners would risk their lives to defend their mom-and-pop stores. The answer is that for many Korean immigrant merchants, their businesses were their lives. They had invested everything in their small businesses, and more important, they had no insurance or were insured by fraudulent overseas companies. In their eyes, they had no choice but to defend their stores at gunpoint.

African Americans and Latinos in South Central Los Angeles

Although the relationship between African Americans and Latinos is not the central focus of this chapter, it is impossible to understand the intergroup dynamics of south central Los Angeles without examining the presence of Mexican and Central Americans in the area. As we pointed out in chapter 1, the demographics of south central have changed dramatically over the past two decades, with the area shifting from a predominantly African American population to one that is nearly half Latino and half Latin American. The presence of Latinos in south central Los Angeles is distinctly different from the presence of Koreans. Whereas Korean Americans come in mainly as merchants, arriving in the morning to open their businesses and then leaving at night, Latinos and African Americans live there as neighbors, sharing the same community facilities and resources. Their competition for jobs and scarce resources is exacerbated by their cultural disparities, ranging from differences in language to music to the way in which people use and decorate their homes.

The controversy over the King-Drew Medical Center epitomizes the tensions between African American and Latinos. It was built in Watts at the behest of African Americans who wanted a medical facility for their community. Today, however, most of the children born at King-Drew are Latino, and many blacks feel that Latinos should not use the facility which blacks fought so hard for. The same sentiment is echoed in the controversies over the presence of day laborers in middle-class black neighborhoods such as Ladera Heights, where neighbors have organized to keep out Latino day laborers.

The competition over jobs is undoubtedly at the heart of much of the friction between African Americans and Latinos in south central Los Angeles, and it has been made even more desperate by the structural changes caused by the impact of globalization and the export of well-paying jobs. It is significant that Latinos arrived in south central Los Angeles just at the time when the area was being hit hardest. As Miles points out in a 1992 article on black-brown relations in Los Angeles, job competition is affected by the fact that white and Asians may prefer to hire Latinos rather than blacks because of the more negative stereotypes of blacks, whereas Latinos are regarded as more amicable and hardworking. In addition, the undocumented status of many Latinos makes them an easily exploitable target for unscrupulous employers who want neither to pay the minimum wage or to provide benefits for their employees. All these factors create a climate of unease between Latinos and African Americans.

These tensions also are political. According to Oliver and Johnson (1984), African Americans tend to be politically more homogeneous than Latinos, voting by blocks and thereby managing to have a more substantial political presence than Latinos do, even though the latter certainly are more numerous. African Americans' relatively greater political success has also led many Latinos to believe that African Americans have garnered more than their fair share of political power. The lack of political trust in African Americans has made it difficult for Latinos and African Americans to work together to address their common concerns, an issue to which we return in chapter 4.

Summary

Despite the Korean American and African American communities' efforts to improve their relations, the situation worsened during the late 1980s and early 1990s. Several factors contributed to the deterioration. Each group had negative perceptions of the other, in addition to their cultural differences. But instead of communicating directly with each other, Korean Americans and African Americans formed their opinions through the media's portrayal of the two groups. Thus, each community's negative stereotypes of the other contributed to the conflict between Korean immigrant merchants and African American residents. The economic restructuring and demographic changes during the 1970s and 1980s also drastically altered racial and ethnic relations and intensified the competition for jobs and scarce resources. The influx of Korean American merchants and Latino residents into south central Los Angeles amid economic despair only increased the antiforeign sentiments of the African American residents. Korean American merchants positioned as a "middleman minority" between the dominant (white) and the subordinate (African American) populations were used as scapegoats and blamed for the economic problems of inner cities. As Pyong Gap Min summed up in his book *Caught in the Middle*, Korean immigrant merchants encountered racial hostility from both the bottom (minority poor customers) and the top (white manufacturers and wholesalers).

3

The Media, the Invisible Minority, and Race

Introduction

Thus far, we have examined structural factors contributing to the interethnic conflicts in the United States. In this chapter, we turn to other external factors that have worsened tensions and/or misrepresented relations between Koreans and African Americans, especially the roles of the media, courts, politicians, and community activists. With the invention of new technologies and the creation of the Internet, the media (print and electronic) now shape, influence, and even control public opinion. "The power of the media lies not only in their ability to reflect the dominant racial ideology, but in their capacity to shape that ideology in the first place" (Omi and Winant 1986, p. 63). But John Irby, president of the California Society of Newspaper Editors, disagreed: "The media's role is not to influence but to report the news and let people make their own decisions" (Stein 1992b, p. 7). Indeed, those working in the media often claim that they are serving the "public interest." But what is this public interest? Who decides what it is? Whose interests do the media represent and protect? And what role did the media play before, during, and after the Los Angeles civil unrest? To what extent did the media's representation of Los Angeles's ethnic relations contribute to the heightened tensions between racial and ethnic groups?

The media, just like any other industry in America, are profit-making businesses. To maximize profits and boost their ratings and sales, newspapers and news stations often seek out controversy, for "controversy means ratings, ratings mean advertising, and advertising means money" (Im 1992, p. 28). Mark Schubb, director of the Los Angeles chapter of Fairness and Accuracy in Reporting, blames directors and station owners for lowering journalistic standards in order to make a profit. Similarly, K. W. Lee, the former editor of the Los Angeles English edition of the *Korea*

Times, accused the *Los Angeles Times* and local TV stations for inflaming racial conflicts in Los Angeles. Lee even went so far as to assert that "the white media is responsible for the acceleration of the City of Los Angeles becoming a Lebanon, and in their own quest for profits and increased audience, pits ethnic groups against one another ("Report Card on the Media," November 12, 1991).

In regard to race relations, the media are a double-edged sword. They have the power to bridge differences and cultivate interracial alliances by holding community forums, launching education campaigns, and accurately reporting racially sensitive events without resorting to racial and ethnic stereotypes. In fact, the English edition of the *Korea Times* and the *Sentinel*, Los Angeles's largest African American newspaper, have tried to mediate racial conflicts between the two communities by promoting positive interactions and exchanging articles and editorials. But the media also can perpetuate racist societal patterns that feed racial conflict, exploitation, exclusion, and the misrepresentation of people of color (Multicultural Collaborative 1996, p. 11). During the 1992 riots, TV news and newspapers exploited racial stereotypes by repeatedly showing distorted, biased, and incomplete images of the city's ethnic minorities (e.g., African Americans, Korean Americans, as well as Latinos and other Asian Americans). For example, given open-ended airtime, the TV news departments turned the uprising into a continuous drive-by shooting, all "Live from Copter Five." Channel 7 (KABC)'s Paul Moyer described those defying police in the streets as "creeps." "Hooligans" was the term used by a newscaster on Channel 2 (KCBS). "Thugs, criminals, and gangbangers" were how someone from Channel 4 (KNBC) described the participants. "Look out for the Crips and Bloods gangs" was the drumbeat on Channel 5 (KTLA). In the end, television stations in Los Angeles benefited from their sensational coverage: the almost-continuous coverage of the riots improved KABC's news ratings by 36 percent (Freeman 1992).

A highly selective image of Korean Americans as gun-toting vigilantes was reinforced by the local TV stations, who repeatedly aired the scene of Korean merchants on rooftops with guns firing seemingly at random. This picture of armed Korean shopkeepers sensationalized the story of Los Angeles's "racial conflict." Rather than reporting on the fears and threats facing Korean American store owners, who were trying to defend their stores from looters and arsonists because the police ignored their calls for help, the media represented Korean immigrants as "lawless vigilantes," failing to inform viewers that they were only reacting to earlier encounters with armed looters.

The TV networks' continual rerunning of security tape that captured the shooting of Latasha Harlins by Soon Ja Du on March 16, 1991, reinforced the vigilante image. Between March 1991 and April 1992, local news stations played the tape of this confrontation over and over. Even though the earlier video footage showed Harlins striking Du several times, the TV stations ran only the part when the teenager collapsed onto the floor. Although we believe that the killing of Latasha Harlins cannot be condoned or justified, the media did not present the incident in its entirety and thus only promoted the image of Korean Americans merchants as violent and racist. As a result, Korean American store owners gained the reputation of being prone to homicidal behavior, shooting at customers at random—especially during the Los Angeles riots (Stein 1992c).

One observer commented that "the presence of TV crews seemed to exacerbate the eerie carnival atmosphere at looting sites" (Institute for Alternative Journalism 1992, p. 121). Also, by disclosing the exact locations of looting sites, the media seemed to invite viewers to participate. "Helicopter journalism" brought the fires and looting into our living rooms, providing a sensationalist and visually exciting view of the chaos and violence. Consequently, "most Americans viewed the riots from the perspective of news helicopters, disconnected from both what was happening on the ground and the actual causes of the unrest" (Institute for Alternative Journalism 1992, p. 10).

Historically, minorities often have been denied access to channels of mass communication, and so their voices have been largely unheard. An Asian American anthology, *Counterpoint*, accurately described Asian American invisibility in the media:

> For Asian Americans, a numerically small minority in the United States, the "public interest" often means no interest. As a rule, sensitivity toward the needs and concerns of Asian Americans has never been a feature of media policy in America, and the best that Asians have come to expect from the major news dailies, television and radio stations is neglect. (Gee 1976, p. 264)

Dean Takahashi, a business writer for the *Los Angeles Times* Orange County edition, also commented on the "media invisibility" of Asian

Americans (Stein 1992a, pp. 13–14). For example, although Asian Americans comprise 10.8 percent of the population of Los Angeles County and Korean Americans suffered disproportionately during the civil unrest, when the *Los Angeles Times* published an opinion poll on August 20, 1993, regarding attitudes toward the Rodney King verdicts and the civil unrest, it failed to include the perspective of Asian Americans.

There are numerous other examples of Asian invisibility in the media before, during, and after the Los Angeles riots. No television stations in Los Angeles interviewed an Asian American in the first seventy-two hours after the Rodney King verdicts were announced. The *Los Angeles Times* and other media ignored a news conference on the second day of the riots when Councilman Mike Woo, Police Commissioner Mike Yamaki, and other Asian American community leaders called for justice for Rodney King. In a *Nightline* interview with Ted Koppel aired on May 1, 1992, only African Americans were invited to express their opinions.[1] It was not surprising, therefore, that Korean Americans were portrayed mainly as rude, disrespectful, and money-chasing merchants. On October 22, 1992, *Nightline* revisited Los Angeles in its program "Aftermath of the Riots." The program covered the Rebuild Los Angeles project but concentrated on the rebuilding of south central Los Angeles. Although many researchers did note the multiethnic nature of the Los Angeles riots, the *Nightline* report failed to mention the rebuilding in the Korean American community and only briefly commented on the Latinos' situation. The program's guests included Jim Brown (a former NFL running back) and a few former gang members, all of them African Americans. Neither Asian Americans nor Latinos were invited to discuss the issues and the future of Los Angeles. The PBS program "Los Angeles Is Burning" (aired on April 27, 1993) acknowledged the presence of Latinos and Korean Americans but spent only ten minutes on them during the half-hour program.

The representations of Latinos during the riots were sensationalist as well. The footage of looting often focused on Latinos, who were referred to as "thugs," "illegal immigrants," and other derogatory or generalized terms. For example, KABC Channel 7 field reporter Linda Mour was interviewed about her experience reporting on looters. "Did you get the impression that a lot of those people were illegal aliens?" asked anchor Harold Greene. "Yes," Mour flatly replied (Institute for Alternative Journalism 1992, p. 45). Reflecting this general anti-Latino and anti-immigrant sentiment, the Immigration and Naturalization Service (INS) conducted sweeps through the riot-torn area, picking up and deporting more than eight hundred persons, nearly all of whom were Latinos (Pastor 1993, p. 4).

The Media's View of Korean–African American Relations

During the 1980s, there were numerous reports of altercations between Korean American merchants and African American customers in Los Angeles, New York, Philadelphia, Atlanta, Chicago, Baltimore, and Washington, D.C., and many observers described the volatility of the Korean–African American relations as "a keg of dynamite ready to explode." The media's role in shaping the public's perception of the relationship between Korean Americans and African Americans was critical. For example, during the twelve months preceding the civil unrest, two-thirds of the *Los Angeles Times*'s articles about Korean Americans discussed the conflict between black customers and Korean American merchants (Chung 1992). At least twenty-six articles dealt with the Harlins-Du case, many of which referred to the "$1.79 bottle of orange juice," suggesting that Korean American merchants did not value of human life, especially that of African Americans. This cruel, shortsighted shorthand for much more complex issues gave some people a reason to target Korean American businesses following the acquittal of the police officers in the King trial (Chang and Oh 1995, p. 135).

Some African American newspapers also contributed to the tensions when they printed editorials accusing the Korean-owned businesses in African American neighborhoods of being a conspiracy perpetuated by the government and Korean Americans working against the African American community. The tensions between Korean Americans and African Americans were first reported in August and September 1983 in a series of articles and editorials published by the *Los Angeles Sentinel*, the city's largest African American newspaper. These editorials charged, for instance, that "the African American community had literally been taken over by Asian businesses in the last five years" (Cleaver 1983b). During the 1980s and the early 1990s, the unrest in the inner cities continued, with several incidents of picketing, boycotts, and violence by African American residents against Korean-owned stores.

Korean–African American Relations in Los Angeles and New York

Before the 1992 Los Angeles civil unrest, the Korean American community in Los Angeles maintained better relations with the African American community than did its counterpart in New York. Several factors were responsible. In New York, several scholars (e.g., H. Lee 1993, Min 1996, Yoon 1997) noted that black nationalist leaders organized boycotts against Korean stores in New York City, with the goal being the black community's economic self-sufficiency. New York's black leaders, such as Sonny Carson and Al Sharpton, called for economic and political self-determination. They believe that only African Americans should own businesses in African American community and argue that Korean-owned stores are impeding African American economic self-determination.

In Los Angeles, black nationalism was not strongly rooted in the African American community. Because most blacks came to Los Angeles area during and after World War II, they did not strongly embrace black nationalism. Moreover, Danny Bakewell, the leader of several boycotts against Korean stores in south central Los Angeles, is a self-proclaimed millionaire and a capitalist. He acknowledged that "what prevented blacks from going into business wasn't just red-lining by white-controlled banks. The reason we don't own most of the stores in our own community is because we have been out-positioned. . . . But the reality, which even black people seem to forget, is that pre-civil rights, we owned all the businesses in our community" (Njeri 1997, p. 134). Bakewell and his followers did not denounce Korean ownership of stores in their neighborhoods but instead demanded that Korean American store owners be more courteous and respectful and contribute to the community's development. Nonetheless, Bakewell skillfully used the "black-people-against-the-world sensibility" to mobilize segments of the African American community against Korean immigrant merchants. He declared, "I don't make any pretense about what I stand for. I stand for the preservation and enhancement of the quality of life for black people. If anybody gets in the way of that, I'm not for that. I'm for eliminating them. Because my mission is to bring home the bacon for black people" (Njeri 1997, p. 131). In addition, although several leaders of south central Los Angeles launched a "Buy black campaign," it did not receive strong support from the residents. This lack of visible and active black nationalist leadership in

Los Angeles may help explain why the relationship between the two communities was better than that in New York City.

The formation of the Black-Korean Alliance (BKA) in Los Angeles also helped reduce tensions in south central Los Angeles, by at least symbolically bridging the gap between the two groups and facilitating communication and understanding between them. Although the BKA was not a leadership or grassroots organization, it was widely recognized as able to facilitate dialogue and dampen conflict between Korean merchants and African American residents in south central Los Angeles. In addition, the Asian Pacific Dispute Resolution Center and the Martin Luther King Dispute Resolution Center worked together to mediate disputes between Korean American merchants and African American customers in south central Los Angeles. In New York, in contrast, despite the several clashes between Korean American merchants and African American residents, no organizations or institutions were established to mediate and/or reduce tensions. For example, before the Red Apple boycott of 1990, there were at least four major boycotts of Korean stores in the New York area,[2] but no organizations or institutions emerged to diffuse or resolve conflicts between Korean merchants and African American residents. In other words, whereas the active involvement of Mayor Tom Bradley's administration helped reduce tensions in Los Angeles, the hands-off approach of Mayor Ed Koch of New York City served to intensify the Korean–African American conflicts there.

Furthermore, both the *Los Angeles Times* and the *New York Times* were influential in the interethnic conflict between Korean immigrant merchants and African American customers in both cities. The controversies surrounding two highly publicized boycotts—of Soon Ja Du's Empire Liquor Market in Los Angeles and the Red Apple in New York—raised many questions about how they were reported and interpreted by the media, the police, politicians, and the courts. How did the politicization of the boycotts and the coverage by the media (i.e., the *Los Angeles Times* and the *New York Times*) affect Korean–African American relations?

The Red Apple and Latasha Harlins Cases

Red Apple is the name of a Korean-owned green grocery store in Brooklyn, New York, the boycott of which began shortly after a dispute between a Haitian immigrant woman, Gisleaine Felissainte, and the Korean American store manager, Pong Ok Jang, on January 18, 1990.[3] It turned out to be one of the most prolonged boycotts in recent history, lasting almost fifteen months.

The facts of the case have been disputed. What happened to Mrs. Felissainte at the Red Apple? Did a store employee assault her, as she claimed? Or was she merely restrained by a Korean American employee shortly after a verbal argument? According to Mrs. Felissainte, "Jang grabbed her, insinuated that she had been shoplifting and slapped her face three times. She said that two store employees punched and kicked her knocking her to the floor and causing injuries that kept her out of work for months" (Lubasch 1991, p. 31).

The manager, Pong Ok Jang, offered an entirely different story, insisting that he and other employees did not assault the woman. Rather, Mrs. Felissainte refused to pay the appropriate amount for the items she wanted to buy. "While she looked in her bag for another dollar, the employee began to wait on the next customer in the long line. Mrs. Felissainte became angry and threw a hot pepper at Mr. Jang. The cashier responded by throwing a pepper back at her. As the argument grew more heated, Mr. Jang tried to calm her down by placing his hand on her shoulder. She sat down on the floor. Police called an ambulance."[4] Initially, Bong Jae Jang, the store's owner and brother of the manager Pong Ok Jang, who had just returned from getting a haircut, was arrested on an assault charge.

No one imagined that the chants of "No respect, no business" and "We will not be moved" would last so long. Neighborhood residents established the Flatbush Frontline Collective to take care of the people on the picket line, and Sonny Carson and the December 12th Movement provided advice to the Flatbush Frontline Collective's boycott of the Red Apple store. (Carson had previously led boycotts of Korean-owned stores in other New York neighborhoods.)[5] On January 30, 1991, a jury acquitted Mr. Jang of the assault charge, and in late May 1991, Mr. Jang sold his store to another Korean immigrant, explaining that he was "too stressed" from the confrontation with protesters and boycotts to continue to run the store.

On March 16, 1991, a Korean American shopkeeper, Soon Ja Du, shot and killed a fifteen-year-old African American girl, Latasha Harlins, in south central Los Angeles. This tragic incident generated anger, disbelief, and shock in both communities. Again, the facts of the incident have been disputed. The security camera showed Du grabbing Harlins's knapsack after she accused her of trying to shoplift a bottle of orange juice. According to the initial police report, Harlins left the juice and the knapsack on the counter and was turning to leave the store when Du shot her once in the back of the head. Soon Ja Du, however, contended that in addition to shoplifting, the teenager was trying to take money from the store's cash register. Before the shooting, after Du grabbed Harlins's knapsack, Harlins hit Du several times, causing her to fall down.

Latasha Harlins's aunt insisted that she "was shot in cold blood without provocation." She also disagreed with the police's contention that the shooting was not racially motivated. Joseph Du, the son of Soon Ja Du, argued that "the shooting was an accident" and that the gun had a hair trigger. He believes that the authorities used his mother as a scapegoat to appease the African American community in the wake of the Rodney King beating scandal (Ford and Lee 1991b, p. B1). (We should note that this incident occurred less than two weeks after the beating of Rodney King by four white police officers. Ironically, video cameras captured both incidents and their footage was frequently juxtaposed on network TV.)

Understandably, the African American reaction to the Latasha Harlins shooting was extremely angry and resentful, feeling that both the police and a Korean American merchant had violated their rights. Shortly after the incident, several Korean-owned stores were reportedly attacked and vandalized by angry crowds (*Korea Times*, March 22, 24, 26, 1991; *Korea Central Daily News*, March 22, 28, 1991). The Koreatown police confirmed that they received several telephone calls from Korean American merchants in south central Los Angeles whose stores were burglarized and vandalized (*Korea Times*, April 3, 1991). Even Chung Lee, a Korean American merchant well known for his good relations with black customers, found himself the target of rumors falsely claiming that his wife was the sister of Soon Ja Du. About twenty-five to thirty people picketed his store, the Watts Market, from March 22 until March 27. Several days later, the store was burned down by an arsonist. Although Lee rebuilt his store, it was burned down again during the 1992 riots.[6] Shortly after the Latasha Harlins shooting incident, the Korean community crime prevention hot line was busy with telephone calls from Korean American merchants who feared retaliation by African Americans. One Korean American merchant reported that an African American patron walked out of the store without paying for a piece of candy, asking, "Are you going to shoot me, too?" (*Korea Times*, April 17, 1991). As a result, tension between the black and the Korean communities was high in south central Los Angeles. Although the Latasha Harlins shooting case did not lead to riots, as many had feared, some observers believe that it did contribute to the destruction of many Korean-owned businesses during the later riots (see Chang 1994a).

Both the Red Apple boycott and the Latasha Harlins shooting occurred after highly publicized and violent encounters between African Americans and whites. In New York, racial tension had been escalating for several years. In December 1984, Bernard Goetz shot and wounded four young black men who asked for a few dollars in a half-empty subway car. Goetz claimed that he fired in self-defense. He was found not guilty on all charges, except that of carrying an unregistered firearm. Tensions continued to mount following the highly publicized Howard Beach (1986) and Bensonhurst (1989) murders, in which white mobs attacked and murdered African American youths who were thought to be invading "their" neighborhoods.

In 1989, the "melting pot" of New York City turned into a "boiling pot" when a white woman executive was raped and severely beaten by several African American youths in Central Park. They were found guilty of sexual assault and rape and received long prison sentences. Together, these highly visible and publicized racial incidents had a profound impact on the lives of whites and African Americans in New York City, and by 1990, it appeared that the city was headed for a "racial war."

Before the Rodney King beating incident, Los Angeles had been promoting itself as an example of a successfully multicultural city. Until David Dinkins was elected mayor of New York in 1989, African Americans had been excluded from the city's ruling coalition. In addition, several accusations by Jewish and African American leaders had strained the relationship between the two groups. Unlike New York City, however, the white liberal Jews and African American coalitions in Los Angeles seemed to be having a positive effect, and they shared political power (Sonenshein 1993). But then the videotape of the Rodney King beating reestablished the racial polarization between whites and blacks. The videotape, which showed King being struck at least fifty-six times by four Los Angeles police officers, and the subsequent trial exposed the police brutality and the pervasive racism against minorities in the Los Angeles Police Department (LAPD). This was not new: the Watts riot of 1965 was ignited by an allegation of police brutality against an African American motorist, and the worsening relations between the police and residents of south central Los Angeles is widely recognized as contributing to the 1992 Los Angeles riots (see Special Advisor 1992, Tucker Committee 1992).

The Role of the New York Times *and the* Los Angeles Times

A close examination of the *New York Times*'s and the *Los Angeles Times*'s reports of the Red Apple boycott in New York and the Latasha Harlins shooting in Los Angeles reveal that they may have heightened the tension and possibly prolonged the incidents. We would argue that more than that, both the *New York Times* and the *Los Angeles Times* acted as agitators. Indeed, the media's representation of African Americans and Korean immigrant merchants are tied to the "racialization" of ethnic relations in America, and we believe that the selective portrayal of the two minority groups (e.g., Korean Americans and African Americans) not only has distorted the social and political reality but also has helped sustain the inequality of majority/minority relationships in American society. The *Korea Times*'s English edition criticized the mainstream media's presentation of facts about the Latasha Harlins shooting incident: "In the eyes of the liberal white media, and African American activists, immigrant grocer Soon Ja Du already stands condemned. . . . To them she is an evil ghetto merchant" (*Korea Times Los Angeles*, July 7, 1991).[7] Although most newspaper accounts of these two events were factually correct, they often distorted or exaggerated the situation through their selective reporting of the incidents, from which critical information was frequently omitted.

The *New York Times*'s reports of the Red Apple boycott and the *Los Angeles Times*'s reports of the Latasha Harlins shooting incident differed in their coverage, use of editorials, and portrayal of Korean Americans and African Americans. The mainstream media, including the *New York Times*, initially failed or refused to cover the boycott of the Red Apple. Although the incident occurred on January 18, 1990, and the boycott began immediately afterward, the *New York Times* did not report the incident or the boycott until early May 1990. In fact, in an editorial, the *New York Post* criticized the *New York Times* for being "irresponsible in its failure to cover the boycott sooner" (*New York Post*, April 23, 1990).

Why did the *New York Times* delay reporting the Red Apple boycott? Perhaps the editors reasoned that New Yorkers were more interested in the Bensonhurst trial and the Central Park rape case than the boycott of Korean-owned stores by African American residents. Four months later, however, the Red Apple story became headline news for the *New York Times* and other media in the New York area. Beginning in May 7, 1990, the *New York Times* ran articles and editorials on the Red Apple boycott for six consecutive days and seventeen times during the month of May. Shortly before this, the Bensonhurst trial ended, with racial tensions running high when the jury failed to convict the white assailants of first-degree murder. But because of the press's extensive coverage of the Red Apple boycott, the racial tensions were diffused, shifting from a white–African American conflict to a Korean–African American conflict (Stein 1992c).

We suggest that the New York media (particularly the *New York Times*) played the "race card" to exonerate a white-dominant establishment of its responsibilities and pitted two minority groups against each other. As a result, Korean Americans became the target of African American anger and resentment. In other words, Korean immigrants were acting as a middleman minority (Blalock 1967, Bonacich 1973). The *New York Times* articles and editorials were sympathetic to the Korean immigrant merchants, portraying them as the passive and powerless victims of an illegitimate boycott by African Americans. In addition, Korean immigrant merchants were seen as displaying the best of American values: Korean immigrants were moving up the economic ladder on their own without assistance from the government (Mydans 1990). Despite language barriers and cultural differences, they were hardworking and determined to succeed:

> Kil Jin Kim's daily schedule: head for the Hunt's point market in the Bronx at midnight and spend the night buying produce he will then transport, unload and arrange an display shelves. He will be busy until 4 P.M. or so, when he will go home, eat and go to bed, to wake up six hours later, at 11 P.M. (Sims 1990, p. B1)

Not only the *New York Times* but also other New York media praised the Korean immigrants' work ethic. In its May 30, 1990, editorial, the *New York Post* praised Mr. Jang (the owner of the Red Apple) as a "hero of the first magnitude for his standing firm against a tough boycott and an ugly campaign." In contrast, the African American boycotters were presented as radicals and racists trying to take advantage of innocent Korean immigrant merchants. A *New York Times* editorial on May 8, 1990, condemned the boycott by saying that "it rode on the tide of ugly, unmistakably racist rhetoric that warrants condemnation from every fair-minded New Yorkers starting with Mayor David Dinkins." Much of the paper's attention was on the leader of the boycott, Sonny Carson. The *New York Times* articles and editorials mentioned several times (May 7, 8, 9, and 10, 1990) that Robert (Sonny) Carson was a convicted kidnapper and racial provocateur. Furthermore, Sonny Carson's own rhetoric and behaviors helped label him as a hatemonger when he repeatedly characterized himself as "antiwhite" and urged the "boycott of all Korean-owned stores." African Americans talked about "people who don't live in our community, don't employ people in our community, don't spend in our community and don't have our best interests at heart" and quoted Carson, that "in the future, there'll be funerals, not boycotts" (Farber 1990). By focusing on Sonny Carson's credibility, the *New York Times* tried to discredit the legitimacy of the Red Apple boycott by praising Korean immigrants as a "model minority" while attacking African American boycotters as "racist."

The *New York Times* articles also introduced its readers to the Korean immigrants' *kye*, or "rotating credit association" (see Light 1972). A *kye* is based on mutual trust and its members' ethnic and homeland ties. Each month each member contributes a fixed amount of money to the association, and each month one person receives the pooled money. This process continues until everyone has received money. *Kye* has been an important social and financial institution helping Korean immigrants raise the necessary initial and operational capital for their business ventures in the United States. The *New York Times's* emphasis on the community's self-help institutions thus served to reinforce the "model minority" image of Korean immigrants.

By praising Korean immigrant merchants as "a shining example" for other minorities to emulate, the press was implying that African Americans had no one but themselves to blame for their failures. This tack was not new. During the late 1960s and the early 1970s, the media depicted Asian Americans as a hardworking "model minority." But both the "model minority" and the "middleman minority" concepts imply racial stratification, creating a three-tier system with whites on the top, Asians in the middle, and Latinos and blacks at the bottom. The not-so-subtle message of the media's coverage of the Red Apple boycott was that African Americans are not victims of white racism but racists victimizing hardworking Korean immigrants who are trying to make a living.

The *Los Angeles Times*'s coverage of the Latasha Harlins shooting case was quite different. The *Los Angeles Times* covered the tragic shooting of Latasha Harlins as soon as it occurred, and its reports were more sympathetic to the African American community than to Korean immigrants. For example, the first report of the shooting was entitled "Slain Girl Was Not Stealing Juice, Police Say"; that is, the merchant was "guilty" of murdering an innocent girl. The next day, March 20, the *Los Angeles Times* published an editorial, entitled "A Senseless and Tragic Killing," excoriating the Korean grocer.

Indeed, the *Los Angeles Times*'s portrayal of not just Soon Ja Du but all Korean immigrant merchants was negative. For example, the *Times* pointed out that "many people who live and work near the Empire Liquor Market [owned by Soon Ja Du] had stopped patronizing the store because the owners often shouted insults at customers and frequently accused them of shoplifting" (Ford and Lee 1991b, p. B1) Although the *Times* had no proof to support these accusations, its negative portrayal of Korean American merchants helped rationalize and justify anti-Korean sentiments and violence.

Unlike the *New York Times*, the *Los Angeles Times* never printed editorials critical of Danny Bakewell, who led the boycott of Korean-owned markets and who has served as president of the Brotherhood Crusade for the last two decades. Instead, the *Los Angeles Times* identified Mr. Bakewell as a "new voice" and a key spokesperson for the African American community in Los Angeles. He appeared on numerous radio and television talk shows and was extensively quoted by the *Los Angeles Times*. In fact, Mr. Bakewell was a master at manipulating the media to get as much exposure as possible. While tensions were increasing between Korean Americans and African Americans, an armed African American robber critically wounded a nine-year-old Korean American girl. Mr. Bakewell acted quickly. The *Los Angeles Times* commented that "the media-savvy Bakewell beat the Korean American community to the punch, announcing that he will hold a news conference of his own today to condemn the shooting. Mr. Bakewell said, 'he was outraged by the shooting'" (Ford and Lee 1991b, p. B1). Although the *Los Angeles Times* knew that Mr. Bakewell was a controversial and provocative leader, it continued to portray him as one of the most important leaders of the African American community by granting him continuous publicity.

Politically savvy opportunists like Bakewell have played a central role in escalating the racial conflict between Korean Americans and African

Americans. They often appeal to black pride and nationalism to promote anti-Korean sentiments and suggest that African Americans should control their own economic destiny by taking over Korean-owned stores. The media are drawn to individuals like Bakewell because their controversial statements make good sound bites, which boost ratings and sales.

By focusing on the Korean–African American conflict, the white establishment is disguising the real issue of institutional racism and racial inequality in America. In this way, the white establishment in New York was able to dismiss the charge of racism by African Americans by accusing them of being "racist" themselves against Korean Americans. In contrast, the *Los Angeles Times* and the Los Angeles District Attorney's Office (whose role is discussed later), may have used the Latasha Harlins shooting case to appease the anger of the African American community in the wake of the Rodney King beating.

Relations between Koreans and African Americans in New York had been simmering since the early 1980s, and rumors were widespread in the African American community that Korean immigrants received special government support to establish businesses in African American neighborhoods.[8] Such rumors may have mistaken Koreans for the Southeast Asians who had recently settled in African American neighborhoods in Oakland, Los Angeles, and other California cities, for these refugees were entitled to receive special federal government support through the Refugee Act of 1981. For example, Southeast Asian refugees were given special preference for public housing, jobs, and other government benefits. Many African American residents resented the preferential treatment, believing it unfair to those who had been in the United States longer. In any event, Sonny Carson and his December 12th movement exploited the anti-Korean sentiment and appealed to African Americans to boycott Korean-owned stores. Fliers distributed throughout the African American neighborhoods proclaimed "Korean Merchants Must Go," and "Jail Koreans Who Assaulted Our Sister." In addition, Sonny Carson and his followers were disappointed and angry over Mayor David Dinkins's refusal to support what they perceived as a "black" agenda, so Carson may have tried to use the boycott as a bargaining chip with the mayor's office by refusing to negotiate to settle the boycott (Chen 1991).

In contrast, a threatened boycott of Soon Ja Du's Empire Liquor Market in south central Los Angeles never was carried out because the store never tried to reopen. Instead, after the shooting, the store remained closed and probably never will open again. Consequently, a boycott would have been meaningless. Instead, Danny Bakewell and his supporters focused on a second shooting incident that occurred three months after the Latasha Harlins case: this was the "John's Market shooting." In this incident, on June 2, 1991, an African American customer, Lee Arthur Mitchell, was shot and killed by a Korean American merchant, Tae Sam Park, in south central Los Angeles. Although it was ruled a justifiable homicide (self-defense), the shooting led to a four-month boycott. In addition, several other Korean-owned stores were boycotted and fire-bombed, and Bakewell and his supporters demanded the permanent closure of Park's store. The boycott ended with an agreement between Bakewell of the Brotherhood Crusade and the Korean American Grocery Association (KAGRO). Under the agreement, protesters ended the boycott of the store, and the store was closed and put up for sale, initially only to African American buyers for the first thirty days.

On March 19, 1991, representatives from the city and county human relations commissions, Mayor Tom Bradley's office, and Korean, black, and Latino groups met at city hall and issued a statement expressing hope that tensions would not escalate. On March 21, Korean community leaders released their own statement in response to the shooting. The Black-Korean Alliance and the mayor's office also issued a joint statement regarding the shooting incident: "We are shocked and appalled at the circumstances surrounding the death of Latasha Harlins. We are deeply concerned that this terrible incident of violence does not aggravate the relationship between African Americans and Korean Americans in our communities" (*Korea Times*, March 27, 1991). Many observers, however, complained that the *Los Angeles Times*'s article "Racial Tensions Blamed in Girl's Death" only inflamed the situation. Although the story may have been factually correct, its title misrepresented the incident, because even the police confirmed that no racial remarks were exchanged during the confrontation between Harlins and Du (*Korea Times*, March 27, 1991). Quick and decisive intervention by the Black-Korean Alliance (BKA) and the mayor's office helped contain the anger and antagonism toward Korean merchants after the Latasha Harlins shooting incident, and the mayor's office helped the two parties negotiate a truce.

Help from the Mayor's Office

One of the striking differences between the Red Apple and the Latasha Harlins cases was the response of the mayor's office to the crisis. When David Dinkins was elected mayor of New York City, he had a reputation of being a consensus builder who could heal racial wounds, and he made it clear that "he was not prepared to take sides in what he said was a 'legitimate' dispute over what had occurred" (Purdum 1990a, p. B1). Mayor Dinkins believed that quiet or behind-the-scenes negotiation was the best way to resolve the boycott. This strategy, however, suffered major damage when Dinkins was unable to control the Bensonhurst incident and the Red Apple boycott.

Both the Korean American community in New York and the mainstream media were critical of Mayor Dinkins's indecisiveness and reluctance to intervene to bring about a quick resolution to the crisis. Feeling pressure from all sectors of the community, Dinkins was finally forced to announce that he was "personally prepared to mediate" and that "he was against the boycott on a racial basis" (Purdum 1990c, p. 1). To mitigate the criticism of him, in April 1990, Dinkins established a fact-finding committee to investigate the causes of the boycott. Four months later, the committee published a report stating that "the boycott is not racial in nature, but it stems from cultural differences." The report essentially blamed everyone except the mayor and even praised the mayor's use of "moral authority" to encourage both sides to negotiate. The report was particularly critical of District Attorney Charles J. Hynes "for moving too slowly in the investigation of the events and the prosecution of pending cases" (Terry 1990, p. B3).

On September 18, 1990, Mayor Dinkins was finally forced to take a public stand when nearly ten thousand Korean Americans rallied in front of city hall to demand more active intervention by the mayor's office. Three days later, Mayor Dinkins visited the Red Apple store, bought about $10 worth of produce, and declared that the boycott should end (Purdum 1990d, p. A1). But the mayor's visit appeared only to intensify the tensions, for shortly afterward, nineteen gasoline bombs were found on the roof of the Red Apple store. In retrospect, many observers wondered why the Mayor Dinkins had not gotten involved much earlier.

Mayor Tom Bradley of Los Angeles was determined not to make the same mistakes. Accordingly, he was quick to get involved in the Latasha Harlins shooting case, assembling leaders of the Korean American and

African American communities in his office. Hoping to resolve this politically volatile situation as soon as possible, the mayor urged them to issue a statement calling for unity and understanding between the two communities.

We should note, however, that otherwise Mayor Bradley did not actually do much to improve the deteriorating relationship between the two communities during his tenure as mayor. Like Dinkins, Bradley also favored "quiet diplomacy" to resolve the tensions in the early 1990s, arguing that this was his style and the most effective way to handle the boycotts. Also, although he took credit for forming the Black-Korean Alliance in 1986, he did little to support its activities (see Chang 1992). For example, the BKA has never received any financial support from the city, although Mayor Bradley repeatedly praised it as one of the city's most important organizations.

Quiet diplomacy seems to be a widely accepted way in which politicians protect their own self-interests. In retrospect, both Mayor Dinkins of New York and Mayor Bradley of Los Angeles were more interested in protecting their own political careers than in resolving their cities' crises.

The Police and the Courts

In the beginning, the New York Police Department and the district attorney's office also were reluctant to get involved in the Red Apple boycott. The police refused to intervene, claiming that they usually did not get involved in civil cases. Although the court issued a preliminary injunction order against the boycotters, ordering them to stay at least fifty feet away from the Red Apple and Church Fruits stores, the police refused to enforce the order. As we pointed out earlier, the mayor's fact-finding committee report was particularly critical of how the district attorney's office handled the boycott. The report stated that "the District Attorney's efforts have contributed to the cynical attitude of the parties and the public toward the justice system and are giving an opening to charges of selective prosecution based on race" (Terry 1990, p. B3). In response, District Attorney Charles J. Hynes criticized the committee's report as "flawed because of inaccuracy and an inaccurate review of the facts and circumstances."

In contrast, the Los Angeles Police Department and the district attorney's office took an "activist" approach to the Soon Ja Du trial. One day after the shooting, the police hastily called a press conference and issued a startling statement. Commander Michael J. Bosti reported that the videotape showed a "scuffle" initiated by Du over the knapsack. His statement clearly implied that the shooting was "unprovoked." In fact, robbery was not mentioned; there was no crime at all, no attempt to shoplift (Ford and Lee 1991a). Later, Deputy District Attorney Roxane Carvajal observed, "It is clear and evident [that] Mrs. Du is a danger to society. Mrs. Du said she was under attack, but the evidence in this case doesn't bear that out" (*Los Angeles Times*, April 8, 1991). It is difficult to understand why the district attorney's office was against Mrs. Du but instead created an atmosphere in which anything less than the conviction of Mrs. Du for first-degree murder would be a miscarriage of justice.

Not surprisingly, some African American politicians exploited the situation to advance their political goals. For example, Diane Watson, a candidate for supervisor, distributed a campaign poster stating "Remember Latasha Harlins: The LIFE of a CHILD MUST be WORTH more than a $1.79 bottle of orange juice" to exploit the anger, rage, and frustration toward Korean Americans and the judicial system. Patricia Moore, a Compton city councilwoman, led a recall campaign against Superior Court Judge Joyce Karlin, who sentenced Soon Ja Du to probation instead of a prison term. (Later, an FBI undercover investigation revealed that Moore used the Harlins case to bolster her own assembly campaign. According to a secretly recorded tape, Moore said, "I hope we recall Judge. But that's not my goal. My goal is to keep the issue alive until the election. So if I can keep this going as an activist and run for the assembly . . . I'll have more notoriety and more publicity than [my opponent] ever will.")

It remains a mystery why the district attorney decided to bring the first-degree murder charge against Mrs. Du when the police knew, based on the security camera videotape, exactly what happened. The videotape clearly shows a heated altercation between Mrs. Du and Latasha Harlins. Contrary to earlier statements by the district attorney's office, the videotape shows that the shooting took place shortly after a heated struggle. Objective observers would agree that the videotape does not reveal premeditation on the part of Soon Ja Du. Accordingly, during the trial, Superior Court Judge Joyce Karlin threw out the first-degree murder charge, and instead, Du was convicted of voluntary manslaughter. In our opinion, first-degree murder was too severe a charge, but probation was too lenient a sentence.

The verdicts handed down to the Korean American grocer in the Latasha Harlins and Rodney King trials added to the perception that the justice system does not serve the interests of African Americans but suggested that the U.S. justice system has a double standard, one for whites and the other for blacks. After African Americans patiently waited for more than a year for justice to prevail, Mrs. Du was found guilty of voluntary manslaughter and sentenced to five years' probation. The lenient sentence once more raised the level of tension between the two communities.

The irresponsible sentencing by an inexperienced superior court judge and the sensational reporting of the anti-Harlins campaign by the local media, including the *Los Angeles Times*, increased tensions and polarized ethnic communities in Los Angeles (see *Los Angeles Times*, November 16, 20, 22, and December 13, 15, 16, 1991). The Soon Ja Du ruling inevitably strained relations between Korean Americans and African Americans. The sentencing became one of the most hotly debated issues in the legal community as well, and it became increasingly difficult for anyone to take a neutral position on the Soon Ja Du ruling.

Summary

In recent years, we have witnessed a dramatic increase in racial tensions and violence in the United States. Demographic shifts, including the "white flight" from urban centers and the greater numbers of Asian and Latino immigrants have contributed to conflicts between minority groups. During the 1980s, the tensions between Koreans and African Americans emerged as one of the most visible and pressing racial issues in America. Unfortunately, the media may have made the problem worse by portraying Korean immigrant merchants and African American residents as adversaries fighting only for their own interests. In New York City, African American boycotters were depicted as racists and radicals, and Korean immigrants were idealized as hardworking and industrious merchants.

In Los Angeles, the *Los Angeles Times* and the police, who referred to the shooting of Latasha Harlins as an unprovoked and a cold-blooded act, helped rationalize boycotts of Korean-owned stores. They described Korean immigrant shop owners as rude, disrespectful money chasers, so

African American residents had legitimate reasons to boycott Korean-owned stores. The leader of the boycott, Danny Bakewell, was praised as a new voice in the African American community who filled a leadership vacuum. The *Los Angeles Times* may have been more sensitive to and sympathetic toward African American issues because African Americans are an important part of the dominant biracial coalitions in Los Angeles politics. In addition, the videotape of the Rodney King beating may have generated more sympathy toward African American concerns.

Regardless of the media's differing sympathies, they played a critical role in shaping the public perception of the Korean–African American conflict. Depending on the prevailing social and political circumstances, the media took sides with either Korean Americans or African Americans. Indeed, the reporting of the boycott by the media became a political act in itself. That is, by pitting Korean American merchants against African American residents, the media diffused the potentially explosive white–African American tension in New York and, to a lesser extent, in Los Angeles.

Public officials also contributed to the conflict's intensification. The district attorney's office brought the charge of first-degree murder against Soon Ja Du despite videotaped evidence showing that the shooting took place in the heat of a struggle. We can only wonder whether the first-degree murder charge was an attempt to appease the African American community and deflect the mounting criticism of the district attorney's office.

As we have seen, Korean–African American relations reveal the complexity of contemporary race relations in America. The courts, politicians, activists, and the media all have manipulated Korean–African American disputes in New York and Los Angeles in an attempt to gain "legitimacy." These agents have often interpreted the disputes to the public in ways that seem to disregard the facts. Even though the events provided an opportunity for the Korean American and African American communities get to know each other and improve their relations, the often misleading representation of Korean merchants and African American residents by the mainstream media not only inflamed the situation but also turned public attention away from the issue of institutional racism in America.

The mainstream media and public figures have the power to influence the racial discourse in America. On the one hand, they can reinforce racial stereotypes, increase racial tension, and heighten the fears of racial and ethnic groups. On the other hand, they can act as official agents of social change, promoting racial healing and harmony. The public must remind these agents of their responsibility to disseminate accurate information and give equal time to the views, concerns, and opinions of all parties. In the process, they could help eliminate racial prejudice and stereotypes.

4

Building Immigrant Communities in Los Angeles

Koreatown and Pico-Union

Introduction

On November 21, 1996, in the Highland neighborhood of Los Angeles, Brenda Hughes, a high school senior, was shot and killed while sitting in the back seat of a car with friends. A fifty-one-year-old market owner had fired his handgun at the car, apparently convinced that Hughes's friends had been shoplifting (*Korea Times Los Angeles*, December 25, 1996–January 28, 1997). Because Hughes was Latino and the market owner, Jo Won Kim, was Korean, this incident was reminiscent of the fatal shooting of Latasha Harlins. Even though many observers feared that the incident in Highland Park might escalate into a public conflict pitting Latinos against Korean Americans, that never happened. The incident did, however, serve as a reminder of the precariousness of social, economic, and political conditions in urban America.

Interventions to improve community relations often are initiated only when relations have deteriorated enough to be visible to those outside the communities (e.g., the occurrence of violent acts or highly inflammatory events). Unfortunately, however, cross-community organizing becomes substantially more difficult when communication difficulties and misperceptions have been allowed to fester to the point of physical violence and confrontation (Diaz-Veizades and Chang 1996). Building a human relations infrastructure in a multicultural urban center, therefore, requires creating positive intercommunity relations before tensions have reached the point of intense verbal or physical abuse. Thus, the reason that we undertook this research project was to prevent conflict by means of cooperation.

In this chapter, we focus on two areas in Los Angeles, one named for the intersection of two streets, Pico and Union, and the other, Koreatown, to examine the immigrant hypothesis and interethnic relations and also the sociocultural, economic, and political issues relating to Latinos and Korean Americans. We decided to concentrate on Korean-Latino relations because of conversations we had with Korean and Central American community activists concerned about the underlying tensions between the two groups, particularly in the Koreatown and Pico-Union areas of Los Angeles. Their concern was based on Korean sweatshop owners' increasingly common practice of hiring undocumented Central American workers and then treating them harshly. Interestingly, the same complaints about Korean sweatshop owners can be heard in El Salvador, where Koreans function as middlemen in the garment industry, much as they do in Los Angeles. In addition, many Central American business owners rent space from Korean landlords, and many residents of Pico-Union live in houses owned by Koreans, creating another possible source of friction.

A survey of eighty-three Central American business owners (Chinchilla and Hamilton 1989) revealed some evidence of animosity toward Asians (the researchers did not ask specifically about Koreans). Some of the respondents complained that the Asians who bought buildings in Pico-Union were raising and, sometimes doubling, the rents. Asians also were buying stores previously owned by Latinos, but maintaining both the products and the clients. Other respondents complained about Asian business practices such as unfair competition. For example, swap-meet vendors complained that Asian suppliers would simultaneously undersell swap-meet vendors while refusing to give discounts for large-volume purchases. Several of the people we surveyed commented that "Latinos buy from Asians, but Asians do not buy from Latinos." At the same time, many in the sample indicated no tension at all with Asians.

Working closely with Korean American and Central American community organizations, we investigated Korean American relations in Koreatown and Pico-Union in order to find out the following: (1) the relations between Korean Americans and Latinos in Koreatown and Pico-Union, (2) suggestions for improving interethnic relations between these two groups, and (3) the common concerns of these two groups.

The Immigrant Hypothesis

In Los Angeles, there are more Korean-owned stores in Latino neighborhoods than in African American neighborhoods. Nonetheless, although African American residents have protested, boycotted, and often come to blows with Korean store owners, Korean store owners in Latino neighborhoods have not encountered the same hostility. Why not? Cheng and Espiritu (1989) proposed the "immigrant hypothesis," that is, that Koreans and Latinos share similar immigrant ideology of hard work, frugality, and the myth of America as a land of opportunity. African Americans, however, believe that Americans have systematically oppressed and exploited them and that other immigrant groups have risen above them at their expense. Accordingly, African Americans may feel hostile toward Korean merchants, whereas Latinos may try to emulate the "success" of Korean merchants.

As immigrants, both Koreans and Latinos face language difficulties and cultural barriers as they adjust to living in the United States. Therefore, they do not feel "shame" or "inferior" when they communicate in "broken English." In fact, it may foster "closeness" when they interact as customer and merchant and/or employee and employer. Indeed, they may sympathize with each other, as they both are aware of the difficulty of immigrant life in America. To what extent is this "immigrant hypothesis" applicable to Los Angeles?

A Brief History of Koreatown and Pico-Union

Koreatown

The first Korean community was formed around Jefferson Boulevard and Normandie Avenue near the University of Southern California (USC) campus. Then, with the large influx of Korean immigrants to Los Angeles after 1965, Koreatown moved from Jefferson Boulevard to Olympic Boulevard. The opening of the Olympic Market in 1969 served as a core around which Korean immigrants could settle, and soon other Korean businesses started to flourish. Today this area is recognized as Koreatown, bounded by Vermont Avenue on the east, Western Avenue on the west, Eighth Street on the north, and Olympic Boulevard on the south. During the 1980s, Koreatown was extended farther north along

Vermont and Western Avenues up to Santa Monica Boulevard, farther east to Hoover Street, farther west to Crenshaw Boulevard, and further south to Pico Boulevard. During this time, Koreans in Los Angeles formed numerous social, economic, cultural, and political associations and organizations to help new immigrants adjust to life in the United States. In Southern California, the Korean American community supports 150 social organizations, 86 alumni associations, 60 Christian churches, 18 Buddhist temples, 4 television stations, 3 radio stations, and several newspapers (Yu 1990).

During the past two decades, Koreatown has grown quickly. In fact, Korean Americans own 33 percent of the property along Western Avenue between Santa Monica Boulevard and Pico Boulevard, most of which was purchased during the 1980s (*Korea Times*, February 23, 1990). One reason for this rapid expansion is the large amount of capital, both legal and illegal, coming from Korea into the United States.[1] The businesses in Koreatown cater mainly to Korean tourists and local Korean Americans. Unlike other Asian enclaves such as Chinatown and Little Tokyo, Koreatown has not been able to attract non-Korean customers and/or tourists. Because the majority of the people who live in Koreatown are Latino, who often patronize Korean markets and gas stations, many of the Korean stores have begun to diversify their products to appeal to non-Korean customers. For example, it is common to find Latino customers buying spicy Korean foods at Korean markets in Koreatown. Nevertheless, Koreatown is primarily an ethnic enclave serving as the center of the Korean immigrant community.

Pico-Union

The geographic boundaries of the Pico-Union area are the Hollywood (101) Freeway on the north, the Santa Monica (10) Freeway on the south, the Harbor (110) Freeway on the east, and Vermont Avenue on the west. Despite the geographic dispersion of Central Americans in Los Angeles mentioned in chapter 1, Pico-Union is the cultural heart of Los Angeles's Central American population, much as Koreatown is the cultural heart of the city's Korean population. Latinos constitute the largest (81.45 percent) group in Pico-Union, followed by Asian Americans (9.8 percent), whites (6.3 percent), African Americans (2.25 percent), and Native Americans (0.24 percent). In addition, the Latino population can be broken down into 41 percent Mexican, 22 percent Salvadoran, and 10 percent Guatemalan (Clinica Monseñor Oscar A. Romero, n.d.).

For several reasons, Pico-Union has been labeled a "zone of need" (see Rodriguez and Vasquez-Rodriguez, 1993). In Los Angeles County, 15.1 percent of the population live below the poverty level, but in the Pico-Union/Westlake area, 35.7 percent of the residents live below poverty level. In regard to women with children under the age of eighteen, 58 percent live below the poverty level, according to a survey conducted by the Clinica Monseñor Oscar Romero, a Central American community organization. Many of the area's larger homes have been subdivided to house several families, resulting in one of the mostly densely populated areas of Los Angeles. The population density of most of Pico-Union can be labeled "greater than three times city average" because its residents live in such overcrowded conditions. The density of the remainder of the area is "over two times the city average," and only a few parts are "above city average." Between 55 to 80 percent of households pay more than 30 percent of their income for housing. Because of the high rents in this area, sometimes twelve to fifteen people live in single one-bedroom apartment, a condition that has led to growing numbers of tent cities in alleys, construction sites, and abandoned lots.

The Pico-Union area of Los Angeles has always been underdeveloped. Like so many marginalized neighborhoods in cities across the United States, Pico-Union lacks job opportunities, day care facilities, and an adequate educational infrastructure and political representation. Together, these factors have led to a high crime rate, underemployment and unemployment, overcrowding, a proliferation of mom-and-pop grocery and liquor stores, gang violence, and prostitution. Pico-Union is indeed a "zone of need."

Nearly half the population of Pico-Union is under 25 years of age, with 25.5 percent under 18, 18.61 percent between 18 and 24, 48.69 percent between 25 and 64, and 4.1 percent over 65. This youthful population has created its own problems, most notably gang violence, drug trafficking, and a greater need for education and day care services. The alienation of Pico-Union's young people is apparent in the fact that 35.3 percent of them drop out of high school.

The Latino population of Pico-Union is both underemployed and unemployed. Whereas the average unemployment rate in Los Angeles is 8.4 percent, it is 10.9 percent for Latino men in Pico-Union. As a result of these high underemployment and unemployment rates, the median family income for Latinos in Pico-Union is $14,761, and the median household income is $25,897, compared with a median income of $34,965 for Los Angeles as a whole. At least 19 to 38 percent more Pico-Union residents are living in poverty than the city average. Yet as writer Joel Kotkin pointed out, Pico-Union is not a typical U.S. urban ghetto with an entrenched welfare population and a dead economy (Kotkin 1997). Rather, the Central American community of Pico-Union has managed to create a bustling center of economic activity, both formal and informal.

The majority of Central Americans in Pico-Union are undocumented and are therefore one of the most vulnerable populations in the labor pool. Furthermore, access to employment possibilities and work training is complicated by the fact that 63 percent of the Latino population in Pico-Union live in households in which no one over the age of fourteen speaks English very well.

Ethnic Enclave: Koreatown and Pico-Union

The Koreatown/Pico-Union area of Los Angeles lies within the broader area known as Westlake, which is just west of downtown Los Angeles. The demographics of the area have changed substantially over the past two decades as a result of the steady increase in Korean and Central American immigration. In fact, Koreatown, despite its name and its function as the center of Korean American activity in Los Angeles, is 70 percent Latino, the majority of whom are Central American immigrants.

Koreatown/Pico-Union is essentially, therefore, a new ethnic enclave that serves the needs of both Korean and Latino (mostly Central Americans) immigrants and refugees. It is an area with both problems and potential. Its potential lies in the entrepreneurial spirit of its Central American, Mexican American, and Korean American residents. Despite high poverty and crime rates, Pico-Union has "a surprisingly vibrant private economy that provides opportunity for newcomers to make it up and often out of the district" (Kotkin 1997, pp. M1–M8). Its problems arise from the historic underdevelopment of the area as well as problems inherent in the clash of immigrant cultures with no common history, language, or cultural practices.

Ethnic enclaves function as the residential and commercial center for new immigrants, but they often mean voluntary separation and involun-

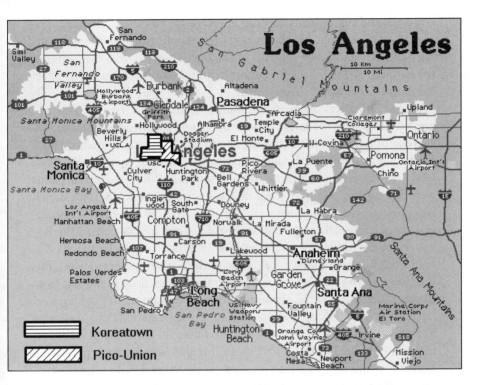

Koreatown

Pico-Union

tary segregation. Although there seems to be no consensus on the definition of an ethnic enclave, scholars do agree on some of its general characteristics. Portes and Bach describe an ethnic enclave as "numerous immigrant-owned business firms which hire numerous co-ethnic employees and spatial clustering of businesses" (1985, p. 203), and Zhou (1992) sees an ethnic enclave as an "institution of accommodation" that functions as both a public service and a private business for the immigrant community.

There are two contrasting views of the functions of ethnic enclaves in American society. The more prevalent view is that an ethnic enclave provides employment opportunities for and eases the sociocultural adjustment of recent immigrants (Min 1988, Portes and Bach 1985, Zhou 1992). The formation of an ethnic enclave is described as a voluntary process in which newly arrived immigrants set up a territory-based community, ethnic enterprises, community and service organizations, and religious institutions. New immigrants thus establish ethnic enclaves to protect themselves from culture shock and to provide themselves with resources and refuge until they can adjust to their new environment. Koreatown, for example, has the important symbolic function of representing Southern California Koreans to the outside world. It is the center of the cultural, social, business, economic, and political activities that affect the daily lives of Korean Americans.

Unlike a typical marginal economy, Koreatown's economy is not greatly affected by the larger American economy. Instead, it is more susceptible to international economic conditions, particularly that of South Korea. For example, Koreatown rapidly expanded during the early 1980s when the American economy was in recession. While industrial plants were closing, the unemployment rate was rising, and the U.S. trade deficit was growing, the Koreatown economy prospered, as shown by its proliferation of minimalls and small businesses. Then in 1997, when the Korean economy suffered a major setback with the sharp decline of the Korean stock market and the devaluation of the Korean currency (won), this hurt Koreatown's economy as well. With the sudden drop in tourists from Korea, Koreatown's travel agencies, hotels, restaurants, and gift shops reported a sizable loss of revenue during the same period, and they have not shown any signs of recovery, despite the rapid growth of the California economy during the mid-1990s. This inverse relationship between Koreatown and the American economy is directly related to the internationalization of labor and capital.

According to a survey conducted by Busicom in 1995, the number of Korean-owned businesses in Koreatown increased by 128 percent between 1984 and 1994. In particular, professional and white-collar businesses grew rapidly. For example, the number of accounting firms, medical offices, and lawyer's offices more than doubled, a trend that suggests the general upward occupational mobility of Korean immigrants. Service- and trade-related businesses also prospered, as the occupational upward mobility of Korean immigrants heightened the demand for quality services.

The second view of ethnic enclaves highlights their dark side as a place where fellow ethnic business owners exploit newcomers. Faced with language barriers, cultural differences, and a lack of employment opportunities outside the ethnic economy, these new immigrants have no choice but to endure harsh working conditions, low wages, and the violation of labor laws (Kwong 1987). Indeed, according to the Korean Immigrant Workers Advocacy (KIWA), many Korean immigrants in Koreatown suffer from the long hours, low wages, sexual harassment, and inhumane treatment by coethnic business owners.[2] The KIWA newsletter reported (October 20, 1997) that for the first month of his employment, a Mr. O received $2.50 an hour which was later increased to $2.80 an hour, still far below the minimum wage of $5.15 an hour. On September 18, 1997, the *Korea Times* related the story of a Korean restaurant worker who was fired from her job. According to the article, "She was terminated on August 17, 1997, after working at S restaurant for about a year." She described the harsh conditions of her work: "I burned my hand more than once from carrying hot dishes containing boiling food. It [still] is painful to even make a fist because the muscle healed without proper medical treatment. I fell several times a day because of the slippery floor at my restaurant. In order to earn $600, I dragged my aching body to work for 10 hours a day, but I was fired in return."

According to KIWA's data, Koreatown contains 283 Korean-owned restaurants, employing 2,000 workers, 70 percent of them Koreans and 30 percent non-Koreans, mostly Latinos (Kang 1998, p. B8). KIWA has launched a major campaign to improve the general working conditions and wages of Korean immigrant workers. For example, on October 17, 1997, claiming deplorable working conditions and low or even unpaid wages, KIWA picketed the Chosun Galbi restaurant, demanding the reinstatement of the restaurant's former cook. Members of the Korean Restaurant Association (KRA) and employees of Chosun Galbi held counterdemonstrations. The KIWA newsletter claimed that "subminimum wages, no overtime pay working conditions, and the employers' failure to carry workers' compensation insurance convinced many community members and even some Korean Restaurant Association members that there really was not a legitimate basis for any disputes" (see *Korea Times*, October 18, 1997). But the disputes between restaurant owners and workers over low wages, unpaid wages, workers' compensation, and better working conditions are likely to continue unless the working conditions of the Koreatown restaurant industry drastically improve.

During the past several years, the disputes between KIWA and the Korean Restaurant Association (KRA) have escalated to the possibility of a lawsuit over the general work environments of Korean restaurants. On October 3, 1996, KIWA and KRA concluded a month of negotiations to resolve the so-called Ho-Dong Restaurant blacklisting incident, which sparked a massive antiblacklisting campaign manifested in a series of public demonstrations and a $500,000 lawsuit against the parties involved in the blacklisting. According to the agreement, KRA will work with KIWA to create a restaurant industry control task force, to establish a "restaurant workers' defense fund, and to improve restaurant working conditions (*Korea Times*, November 9, 1996). Although KIWA conducted seminars in twelve Korean restaurants, many Korean restaurant owners refused to permit them (*Korea Central Daily*, August 15, 1997). Furthermore, KRA claimed that the former president signed the agreement with KIWA without consulting its members; therefore, KRA will not contribute money to establish a restaurant workers' defense fund. On September 24, 1997, KRA's attorney, Richard Kim, held a press conference at which he demanded that KIWA "stop the labor law seminars at member restaurants, stop picketing and boycotting." He insisted that disputes be resolved through lawyers and that KIWA return the $10,000 restaurant workers' defense fund to KRA. In response, Roy Hong, KIWA's executive director, stated, "If KRA really wants to talk, then they should not demand anything from us. And we cannot accept KRA's demands" (*Korea Central Daily*, September 23, 1997). Kim maintained that "we cannot communicate with these people [KIWA] any more. We have to rely on the law. By next week, we are going to file a lawsuit against KIWA at the regional court for disrupting businesses, illegally entering, and defamation" (*Korea Times*, October 18, 1997).

On September 19, 1997, an editorial in the *Korea Times* criticized KRA for neglecting its obligation to protect the welfare of its restaurant workers and called for a reconciliation between KIWA and KRA in order to improve working conditions in Koreatown restaurants. On September 18, 1997, the *Korea Central Daily* criticized KRA's attorney, Richard Kim, for making the dispute worse with his inflammatory remarks. In any case, these disputes serve to demonstrate that the Koreans in Koreatown are not a homogeneous group with shared interests and experiences.

Although Los Angeles's Central American community does not have the capital resources of the Korean community, Central Americans have been able to open hundreds of small businesses. These businesses can be divided into three general types: formal establishments that have traditionally served a white clientele, formal establishments that serve primarily other Latinos and Central Americans, and informal businesses such as street and market vendors. The formal businesses range from small restaurants to large export houses to small auto repair shops (Chinchilla and Hamilton 1989). According to a study of Central American business owners, the primary source of capital for business ventures comes from

TABLE 4.1
*Ethnic Orientation of Central American
Businesses in Los Angeles*
(n = 83)

Speak mostly Spanish to customers	85.5%
Ethnic/national origin of customers	
National group	32.5
Other Central American	26.5
Other Latino	34.1
Ethnic nationality of employees	
National group	34.9
Other Central American	18.1
Other Latino	13.1
Origin of Supplies	
National Group	10.8
Other Latino	37.3

SOURCE: Chinchilla, N., and N. Hamilton, *Central American Enterprises in Los Angeles,* New Directions for Latino Public Policy Research Working Paper no. 6, Center for Mexican American Studies, University of Texas at Austin, 1989.

personal savings or family contributions. This reliance on personal capital contributes to Central Americans' belief that Asians are able to run more profitable business establishments because of the perception that they buy cooperatively. We found, in our own work, that this belief translated into the Latino respondents' admiration for the "unity" they see in the Korean community.

These Central American businesses offer job opportunities and at the same time create a feeling of solidarity in a somewhat isolated community. Ethnic-owned businesses, both Korean and Central American, provide a sense of identity and pride. Unlike Korean-owned businesses, which serve non-Korean communities, Central American businesses, as indicated in table 4.1, have historically served primarily Central American or other Latino clientele. Next we examine another dimension of ethnic enclaves: economic and social Korean-Latino relations.

Methodology

For our survey, teams of Korean- and Spanish-speaking interviewers collected data through one-on-one interviews. In Koreatown, the interviewers spoke with the owners of small businesses, customers, and merchants in swap meets, and individuals on the streets. In the Pico-Union area, interviews were conducted at MacArthur Park (a centrally located park where many individuals and families congregate on weekends), in laundromats, in mom-and-pop stores, and on the street. The interviewees were paid for participating in the study.

We interviewed a total of 114 Koreans and 83 Latinos. Of the Koreans interviewed, 51.8 percent were male and 48.2 percent were female, ranging in age from twenty-four to eighty; 97.4 percent identified themselves as Korean and 94.7 percent named Korean as their first language. The Latino sample was more diverse. Of those we interviewed, 51.8 percent were male and 48.2 percent were female, ranging in age from twenty-one to eighty-one. In regard to ethnicity, the Latino sample was 39.8 percent Mexican, 31.3 percent Salvadoran, 14.5 percent Guatemalan, 8.4 percent Honduran, and 6 percent other.

We also should note that the work presented in this chapter was a collaboration of the Los Angeles Multicultural Collaborative, Korean American and Central American community organizations, and researchers from the University of California. In this connection, Gary Phillips of the Los Angeles Multicultural Collaborative convened a meeting of Korean American and Central American community organizations. Present at this meeting were representatives from the Korean Immigrant Workers' Advocate (KIWA), Clinica Oscar Romero, Central American Resource Center (CARECEN), Mexican American Legal Defense and Education Fund (MALDEF), Coalition for Humane Immigrant Rights, and other groups. We based the contents of this survey, and our method of collecting data, on our conversations with these community organizations. We undertook the project with the specific goal of gathering information that could help in the development of cooperative community ventures between the Korean American and Latino American residents of Koreatown and the Pico-Union area.

Korean-Latino Relations

Koreatown and Pico-Union are located geographically next to each other, so the two areas have sizable overlapping borders where they share public, commercial, and residential spaces. But the problems facing the residents of Koreatown and Pico-Union are amplified by the lack of cooperative relations between the two communities' residents. For example, residents

TABLE 4.2
*Where Do You Normally Interact with
Koreans and Latinos?*

	Koreans (%)	Latinos (%)
Neighbor to neighbor	26.3	15.9
In stores	48.3	57.6
On the job as employer	42.9	14.9
On the job as employee	12.3	8.8
In business transactions	25.5	30.4
On the street	64.8	30.2

TABLE 4.3
*How Would You Describe Interactions between
Koreans and Latinos?*

	Koreans (%)	Latinos (%)
Very favorable	0.9	18.2
Favorable	12.3	35.1
Neutral	67.5	20.8
Uncomfortable	14.9	15.6
Very uncomfortable	2.6	5.2

separate themselves mainly by cultural differences, such as those between Central Americans and Mexican Americans (and indeed among different Central American groups) and between Korean Americans and Central or Mexican Americans. Only a concerted effort, led by community organizations, could bridge these differences to reach some sort of cooperation.

To understand the context in which Korean-Latino interactions take place, we asked the survey participants to indicate where they usually interacted with members of the other community. Their responses are presented in table 4.2 and indicate that the two groups interacted most frequently on the street or in stores.

When asked how they would describe Korean-Latino interactions in general (table 4.3), only a minority of the respondents in both groups said that the interactions were uncomfortable or very uncomfortable, with the majority in the Latino sample reporting the interactions to be favorable and the majority in the Korean sample answering that the interactions were neutral. The respondents were then asked open-ended questions to find out why they felt the way they did about Korean-Latino interactions (i.e., why they felt that the interactions were either positive or negative). Of the 65 Latino respondents, 47 percent said that their interactions with Koreans were positive. And of that 47 percent, 31 percent stated that

Koreans were friendly, 9 percent that Koreans were good and/or fair people, 5 percent that relations were positive because Koreans made an effort to speak Spanish, and 2 percent that they viewed Koreans positively because they believed Latinos and Koreans had things in common. Twenty-eight of the Latino respondents provided neutral responses: 11 percent stated that they did not have many interactions with Koreans, 9 percent that relations between Koreans and Latinos were strictly confined to business relations, 5 percent that sometimes relations were good and sometimes bad, and 3 percent that the only problem was with language and communication. Nineteen percent of the Latino respondents had negative things to say about Korean-Latino relations: 17 percent indicated that Koreans were not friendly, were rude, and kept to themselves, and 2 percent stated that Koreans were difficult to work for. Forty-seven Korean participants responded to the question about Korean-Latino relations. Thirty-seven percent provided positive descriptions of their interactions with Latinos, stating that Latinos were friendly and hospitable (17 percent), that Latinos were innocent (6 percent), that Latinos were diligent and hardworking (6 percent), that there were no tensions between Koreans and Latinos (4 percent), and that there were similarities between Koreans and Latinos (4 percent). Reflecting the responses provided in table 4.3, 59 percent of the Korean respondents indicated that relations between Koreans and Latinos were neutral. Of this 59 percent, 34 percent stated that they did not have communication or interactions with Latinos, 15 percent that relations were only business related, 4 percent that the two groups had different values, 6 percent that they had no interest in interacting with Latinos, and 2 percent that their relations were sometimes good and sometimes bad. Eleven percent of the respondents had very negative things to say about Korean-Latino relations, with 9 percent stating that Latinos were dishonest and dirty and 2 percent that they hated Latinos.

Responses to the next survey question helped elucidate some of the preceding answers. When asked whether Koreans and Latinos had anything in common, slightly more than 50 percent of each group answered yes. But more than one-third of the Latinos and roughly one-quarter of the Koreans answered no (table 4.4). In addition, the participants were asked to list those things that they believed Koreans and Latinos had in common (table 4.5). What is striking here is the number of similar responses by the two groups. In general, Koreans and Latinos were aware of how the two groups' cultures converged, although the Latinos perceived a greater commonalty between themselves and Koreans than the Koreans

TABLE 4.4
Do Latinos and Koreans Have
Anything in Common?

	Latinos (%)	Koreans (%)
Yes	51.2	56.1
No	35.4	21.9
Don't know	11.0	21.1

TABLE 4.5
Things That Latinos and Koreans
Have in Common

	Latinos (%) (n = 36)	Koreans (%) (n = 54)
Customs and Values	36	41
Family Values	39	14
Hard Workers	44	4
Immigrants and Language	36	11
Environment and Contact	8	13
Physical Similarities	0	7
Minorities and Persecution	0	15

did. It is interesting to look at the two groups' definitions of common themes. Under the category "Customs and Values," the respondents listed such things as a love of food and music. The "Environment and Contact" category included the mere fact of proximity to each other or similarities in living conditions. Under "Family Values," the respondents noted such concepts as "respecting the family" or "having big families." For the "Hard Workers" category, both groups said they believed that both Koreans and Latinos were hardworking. The "Immigrants and Language" category included similarities such as both groups were immigrants and both either spoke English as a second language or not at all. For "Minorities and Persecution," the respondents reported similarities based on the fact that both groups were minorities, meaning that they both were struggling with the society at large. Finally, the "Physical Similarities" category covered height, color of skin, and the like.

The respondents were then asked about their knowledge of various aspects of the other community's culture. In each group, most of them indicated that they had very little to no knowledge of the other group's language, history, music, food, or religion. This finding is not surprising given the immigrant status of both groups as well as the probability that very few Latino or Korean immigrants envisioned themselves interacting with members of the other group upon their arrival in the United States.

TABLE 4.6
*Do Korean and/or Latino Immigrants Have a
Positive or Negative Impact on Your Neighborhood?*

	Latinos (%)	Koreans (%)
Positive	72.0	28.1
Negative	11.0	33.3
Don't know	17.1	35.1

TABLE 4.7
*Examples of Koreans' Positive Impacts on
Latino Neighborhoods*

Number of Latino Responses = 46

Create jobs and businesses	48%
Are ambitious and hardworking	15
Personality	13
United	11
Bring money	4
No crime	4
Their culture	2
Are immigrants like us	2

TABLE 4.8
*Examples of Latinos' Positive and Negative Impacts
on Korean Neighborhoods*

Number of Korean Responses = 61

Provide cheap labor	28%
Are customers at Korean stores	20
Hard workers	7
Useful to Koreans	3
Crime	33
Dirty	20
Bad influence in neighborhood	7
Can't communicate	3
Gangs	3
Negative preconceptions of Latinos	3
Job competition	2
Envy Koreans	2

Generally the Koreans appeared to know more about Latino culture than Latinos did about Korean culture. The reason was mainly that Koreans were more often stores owners and therefore had a greater need to know their clients—Latinos and others—in order to succeed.

Next, we looked at the communities' perceived impact on each other. First, we asked the participants in each group whether they thought the other group had a positive or negative impact on their neighborhood (table 4.6). Nearly 75 percent of the Latinos believed that Koreans had a positive impact on their neighborhood, whereas the Koreans were nearly equally divided among having positive feelings, negative feelings, and no opinion about having Latinos in their community.

We then asked the groups to explain their answers (tables 4.7 and 4.8). The responses to this question reflected the functional aspects of relations between the two groups. In an interesting juxtaposition, the largest number of Latino responses (48 percent) indicated that the Koreans provided jobs, whereas the largest number of Korean responses (28 percent) stated that the Latinos provided a cheap source of labor. On the whole, the Latino responses regarding the Koreans were more complimentary than the Korean responses regarding the Latinos. All the Koreans' positive responses centered on the usefulness of Latino immigrants to the Koreans' entrepreneurial goals.

Neighborhood Issues and Concerns

Liquor Stores

When we initially sat down with members of Latino and Korean community organizations, we were told that issues regarding liquor stores, street vendors, and day laborers were responsible for most of the conflict between the two communities. As in many other economically marginalized neighborhoods of Los Angeles, the Latino area of Pico-Union has a disproportionately high number of liquor stores, many of which are owned by Koreans. Therefore, when asked whether liquor stores were a problem, it was not surprising that 76 percent of the Latinos answered yes, in contrast to 23 percent of the Koreans. It is also noteworthy that 31 percent of the Koreans replied "don't know" to whether a problem even existed (table 4.9).

What should be done about liquor stores? When asked specifically what should be done about them, 31 percent of the Latino respondents thought that the liquor stores should be "closed down"; 20 percent suggested greater enforcement of the no-selling-to-minors law; and 13 percent favored enforcement of the laws regarding drugs and prostitution (table 4.10). Thirty-five percent of the Korean respondents recommended not selling alcohol; 17 percent mentioned the idea of improving customer relations; and 13 percent advised reducing the number of business hours (table 4.11).

TABLE 4.9
Are Liquor Stores a Problem?

	Latinos (%)	Koreans (%)
Yes	75.9	22.8
No	21.7	46.5
Don't know	1.2	30.7

TABLE 4.10
What Should Be Done about Liquor Stores?

Numbers of Latino Respondents = 54

Close them down	31%
Don't sell to minors	20
Regulate problems around stores (i.e., gangs, violence, drugs, prostitution)	13
Alcohol itself is the problem	9
Put them in out-of-the-way places	6
Prohibit sale of alcohol	4
Create alternative types of businesses	4
Change advertising regarding alcohol	4
Put a sales tax on alcohol	2
Sell things other than alcohol	2
Change hours of operation	2

TABLE 4.11
What Should Be Done about Liquor Stores?

Number of Korean Respondents = 23

Don't sell alcohol	35%
Improve customer relations	17
Reduce business hours	13
Decrease number of stores	9
Get rid of them	4
Strengthen regulations on sales	4
Don't sell to minors	4
Increase police presence	4
Obey laws regarding alcohol	4
Problem is with customers, not stores	4

Street Vendors

Street vendors were rumored to cause significant tensions between Koreans and Latinos because of their illegal status and because they sometimes took business away from Korean-owned stores. When asked about the impact of street vendors on their neighborhoods, the two groups' responses were the most divergent in the survey (table 4.12). Sixty-two percent of the Koreans viewed street vendors as bad for the community; 34 percent were unsure how they felt; and none saw street vendors in a positive light. In contrast, 72 percent of the Latinos said that vendors had a positive impact on the neighborhood. When asked to explain their views, several Latinos mentioned that occasionally street vendors had given them free food when they were in need and that vendors allowed them to pay later for food when they were short on cash (table 4.13). An equal-but-opposite effect might explain the Koreans' negative view of street vendors as outsiders who posed a threat to their image of the neighborhood (table 4.14). Although street vendors

TABLE 4.12
*Are Street Vendors Good or Bad for
Your Neighborhood?*

	Latinos (%)	Koreans (%)
Good	71.6	
Bad	16.0	62.3
Don't know	12.3	34.2

TABLE 4.13
Why Do You Feel This Way about Street Vendors?

Number of Latino Respondents = 67

Have a right to work and earn money	34%
Sell good products at good prices	13
Are friendly	10
Don't harm anyone/honest work	9
Convenient	9
Provide a community service	9
Part of customs and culture	3
Provide business	1
Sell dirty food	10
Take away from legal businesses	6
Hang out with drug dealers	3
Obstruct traffic	3

TABLE 4.14
Why Do You Feel This Way about Street Vendors?

Number of Korean Respondents = 49

Dirty	53%
Bad neighborhood image	33
Negative impact on other businesses	12
Crime	10
No ethics	4
Traffic problem	4
No regulation of food	3
Pushy attitudes	1

TABLE 4.15
Are Day Laborers Good or Bad for
Your Neighborhood?

	Latinos (%)	Koreans (%)
Good	72.3	17.5
Bad	11.4	26.3
Don't know	11.4	53.5

TABLE 4.16
Why Do You Think Day Laborers Are Good or Bad
for Your Neighborhood?

Number of Latino Respondents = 54

They are working and earning money.	52%
They help the community.	9
They work hard for less pay.	7
They behave well.	6
They help create work.	6
They are good people.	2
They provide a service.	2
They are part of the culture.	2
They are discourteous.	4
They are illegal.	2
Some sell drugs.	2

TABLE 4.17
Why Do You Think Day Laborers Are Good or Bad
for Your Neighborhood?

Number of Korean American Respondents = 41

Source of cheap and available labor	37%
Hard workers	12
Crime	34
Dirty	17
Bad image	7
Illegal	5
Obstruct traffic	5
Make community look bad	2
Drinking problem	2

could not compete with the Korean-owned stores, Korean business owners nonetheless regarded them as a threat. The striking differences in the two groups' responses may be explained in large part by the fact that most street vendors are Latino. They thus are members of the Latino culture and community, and they provide a convenient and affordable service, including a kind of informal social welfare.

Day Laborers

Day laborers have also been a source of controversy in Pico-Union and Koreatown. Day labor concerns are by no means unique to Pico-Union but are part of the fabric of many neighborhoods with a high percentage of undocumented workers. Day laborers often congregate on street corners or in parking lots of hardware and "home-improvement" stores waiting for employment. When asked whether day laborers pose a problem to their neighborhood, the responses from Latinos and Koreans were quite different (table 4.15). The majority of Latinos indicated that day laborers were good for their neighborhoods, whereas more than 50 percent of Koreans said that they did not know whether or not they were good or bad for their community. The percentages of the two groups' responses are given in tables 4.16 and 4.17.

Again, the principal purpose for our project was to find out how best to address joint community concerns and to create cooperative relations between Koreans and Latinos who live in the Pico-Union/Koreatown areas. When we asked Latinos and Koreans whether they would be willing to join in tackling community problems, the Latinos, once again, conveyed an eagerness surpassing that of the Korean respondents (table 4.18). Whereas 90 percent of the Latinos were open to the idea of working

TABLE 4.18
Should Koreans and Latinos Work Together?

	Latinos (%)	Koreans (%)
Yes	90.2	68.4
No	3.7	6.1
Don't know	4.9	21.1

TABLE 4.19
On Which Issues Would You Like to Work with Latinos or Koreans?

	Latinos (%)	Koreans (%)
Economic development	61.4	8.8
Health care	61.4	13.2
Child care	62.7	4.4
Education	68.7	7.0
Crime prevention	74.7	28.9
Low-cost housing	65.1	0.9
Public transportation	55.4	0.9
Alcohol/drug prevention	71.1	5.3
Anti-immigrant legislation	63.9	1.8

with the Koreans, only a bit more than half (68 percent) the Koreans could imagine joining forces with Latinos for the sake of the neighborhood. We next wanted to know how Koreans and Latinos together might improve the community (table 4.19). Once again, Latinos appeared more willing to work with Koreans on a range of community issues than Koreans were to work with Latinos. Of the nine community issues listed, Koreans were most willing to work with Latinos to prevent crime, though only 29 percent, compared with 75 percent of Latinos. The Koreans showed even less interest in the other categories. By comparison, the Latinos' responses were much more positive.

Summary

The geographical proximity of the Latino and Korean communities, combined with the fact that as immigrants, they face many of the same obstacles to community development, suggest that Latinos and Korean Americans may be able to develop mutually beneficial social, political and economic relations. Unfortunately, however, Latinos and Korean Americans are not engaged in the kinds of interactions through which they can develop the trust necessary to build constructive alliances and relationships.

In general, Korean Americans seem to have mixed attitudes toward Latinos. For example, many Korean Americans stated that "Latinos are hard workers, but they drink too much." and "They are good people, but they come from low educational background." Because in Korea, a person's status is often determined by his or her educational attainment, it is not surprising that some Korean Americans believe they are superior to Latinos. At the same time, however, they recognize that Latinos are an important source of cheap labor and/or an important customer base for their businesses.

The Latino immigrants in Pico-Union that we surveyed generally admired the Koreans' work ethic and wanted to emulate them. As Cheng and Espiritu (1989) proposed in their "immigrant hypothesis," these perceptions may explain the lack of ethnic conflict between Latinos and Korean Americans. In addition, many Latinos believe that Korean Americans have a "positive" impact on their neighborhoods because Korean-owned businesses provide employment opportunities for Latino immigrants, a view that differs significantly from that of African Americans.

Perhaps these different attitudes can explain the different reactions of African Americans and Latinos to the two shooting incidents involving Korean immigrant entrepreneurs mentioned at the beginning of this chapter. The shooting incidents that took place in March and June 1991 in African American neighborhoods led to boycotts of Korean stores by the African American residents. But the responses of Latino residents to the shooting of a Latina teenager by a Korean shop owner did not lead to public conflict between the Korean and Latino communities. In fact, many of the residents of Highland Park did not condemn Mr. Kim for shooting Brenda Hughes in October 1996. Instead, they circulated a petition to help reduce his bail during the prearraignment hearing. It is important to note that Mr. Kim lived in Highland Park and had a close relationship with his customers and also was from the same working-class background as his customers. In contrast, Soon Ja Du did not live in south central Los Angeles and was not close to her customers.

Liquor stores, day laborers, and street vendors remain the most volatile and divisive issues among Korean Americans, Latinos, and African Americans. After the 1992 Los Angeles civil unrest, African American activists and politicians began a campaign to reduce the number of liquor stores in south central Los Angeles, arguing that liquor stores invited criminal activities and contributed to the neighborhood's deterioration. This controversy may also have contributed to the Pico-Union residents' unfavorable view of liquor stores.

In regard to street vendors, during a public hearing, several speakers representing home owners' and merchants' associations voiced their opposition to legalizing street vending in the city of Los Angeles. For example, "Greg Smith, a spokesman for a group of African American merchants, said, vendors who do not have rent and other overhead costs can unfairly discount the prices for their goods. Ryan Song, executive director of Korean American Grocers Association (KAGRO), stated that illegal vendors do not pay taxes and cut into business of merchants who do" (Rainey 1993, p. B3). However, many Latinos view street vending as a legitimate way to make a living in America. Just as swap meets are a familiar and common form of business for Korean Americans, so street vending is in Central America and Mexico. Indeed, street vending is also common in Korea. In any case, the controversies over liquor stores, street vendors, and day laborers will remain obstacles to forming cooperative relations among the Korean American, Latino, and African American communities.

Although the majority of Korean respondents had neutral attitudes toward their relations with Latinos, many also have expressed concern about the lack of positive interactions with the Latino community. In general, Latinos were willing to work with Korean Americans to improve their neighborhoods and intergroup relations, and Korean Americans were willing to work together to prevent crime.

Cheng and Espiritu (1989)'s immigrant hypothesis attributed the relative absence of interethnic tensions between Latinos and Koreans to their shared immigrant status and belief in an "immigrant ideology." Our study partially confirms this. Indeed, as newcomers to the United States, Koreans and Latinos share similar experiences, such as a language barrier, cultural differences, employment discrimination, and anti-immigrant scapegoating. These common problems helped reduce tensions between the two groups. And yet tensions could grow between two groups unless they actively try to solve their interethnic conflicts.

Both groups expressed a desire to work together to foster trust and better interethnic relations. They need a public space in which they can interact more constructively and develop a mutual trust (Oliver and Grant 1995). For example, schools and churches could be sites of meaningful interaction between the two groups. Many Korean American and Latino children attend the same schools in Koreatown and Pico-Union. Furthermore, many Central Americans are Christians, and approximately 70 percent of Korean Americans are regular churchgoers. The success of any interethnic coalition depends on how serious the various groups are about engaging in activities that foster trust and mutual respect.

5

Building Cross-Cultural Coalitions

*The Black-Korean Alliance (BKA) and
the Latino-Black Roundtable (LBR)*

With the increase in interethnic conflict around the globe and
the greater significance of ethnic group membership, communities
around the world are faced with the question of whether it is possible for
ethnically defined groups to coexist peacefully or whether they are
doomed to continuously escalating ethnic friction. Moreover, we must
ask whether these disenfranchised communities, many of which are communities of color, can work together to change the underlying socioeconomic and sociopolitical conditions that often form the backdrop of interethnic tensions. In other words, the challenge for America may be less
to harmonize these groups' relations than to mobilize their cooperation
for economic and political advancement (Multicultural Collaborative
1996, p. 38). How these questions are answered will define the future for
many societies around the globe, particularly for nations like the United
States, which were founded on culturally diverse immigration.

Some analysts believe that maintaining cultural uniqueness is divisive
and eventually balkanizes societies into culturally separate and economically competitive factions (Gitlin 1993a and b, Schlesinger 1991). Other
writers envision societies in which culturally diverse groups retain their
unique ethnic heritage while simultaneously cooperating in social, economic, and political interactions (Banks 1986, Duster 1990, Glazer 1993).
Indeed, the creation of political, social, and economic alliances among
culturally distinct groups may facilitate the development of cooperative
multicultural pluralism (Chang 1995, Sonenshein 1993). The Los Angeles
civil unrest of 1992 made us realize the complexity of interethnic and
racial relations in America. The challenge is for groups to overcome their
negative perceptions of one another and to form coalitions. In fact, coalition building has emerged as the most viable option for the Los Angeles's

rebuilding process. Therefore we ask, what types and forms of coalition building? With whom? On what terms? For what purposes? Under what conditions do coalitions succeed or fail? How can we set aside racial, ethnic, and class differences to find common ground? Obviously, no single theory can provide a satisfactory analysis of the complex and evolving issues related to interminority relations in America, so in the following section, we discuss several theories of coalition building and their shortcomings and strengths. Finally, we suggest an alternative model for building multiracial and multiethnic coalitions.

Methodology

The goals of the proposed coalitions, plus the fact that they would be composed of unfamiliar coalition partners, required that we use an exploratory rather than a confirmatory approach. As we pointed out in the previous chapter, the Korean and Latino communities have not yet tried to form a coalition. In contrast, in Los Angeles between 1986 and 1992, experimental interethnic coalition groups were established to reduce tensions between African Americans and Latinos (the Latino-Black Roundtable, LBR) and African Americans and Korean Americans (the Black-Korean Alliance, BKA). We thus examined the BKA's and the LBR's formation and activities and the reasons for their demise. Our data consist of meetings' minutes, written reports of the coalitions' functions, information from interviews, and a review of the preexisting literature on the Black-Korean Alliance and the Latino-Black Roundtable (Chang 1992, Kim 1995, Regalado 1994). We chose our interviewees in consultation with the staff of the Los Angeles Human Relations Commission (LAHRC) and members of the BKA and LBR.

We interviewed eight members of the BKA: three African American males, one African American female, two Korean American females, and two Korean American males. All were active members of the BKA, and three had served as cochairs at one time. We also interviewed eight members of the LBR: two Latinas, two Latinos, three African American males, and one African American female. All of them also were active members of the LBR and had served as cochairs at one time. Since the number of each coalition's active members did not usually exceed twenty, we were able to interview approximately one-third of the core membership of each organization. Finally, we interviewed the two human relations staff involved in developing the BKA and LBR.

Theories of Coalition Building

Coalition research has usually focused on coalitions with concrete goals such as winning political office, passing legislation, or pushing for higher wages (see, e.g., Budge and Keman 1990, Gamson 1961, Jackson and Preston 1991, Wilke 1985), and Brecher and Costello (1990) discuss and exemplify how coalitions among communities of color are becoming a permanent aspect of labor-management interactions and electoral politics (also see Anderson 1992, Chang 1992, Henry 1990, Sonenshein 1993, Uhlaner 1991).

Coalition theories tend to assume individualistically based and rationalistic motivations for coalition membership and formation (Adrian and Press 1968, Chertkoff 1975, Gamson 1961, Komorita 1974, Komorita and Chertkoff 1973, Riker 1962). Although it is true that individuals join coalitions to maximize individual payoffs, for most members these payoffs cannot be quantified solely in individualistic terms. Rather, the payoffs are collectivist in nature and related to the desire to advance the group's needs. In fact, membership in a coalition may result in negative payoffs in terms of the amount of time spent and the potential for being alienated from one's community (i.e., being labeled a traitor). These individual discomforts are acceptable, however, in light of the greater collective good that members anticipate the coalition can deliver. The greater relative importance of group versus individual need generally characterizes those coalitions that represent cultural groups with collectivist/independent value systems rather than individualistic/independent value systems (see Markus and Kitayama 1991). Several models or approaches have been used for building human relations, interest-based, neighborhood-based, and issue-based coalitions.

The Human Relations Approach

Many people join coalitions for altruist reasons, for example, during the 1960s, the civil rights movement, antiwar protests, and the Third World Liberation Front. These reasons are characteristic of the human relations model approach to coalition building, especially those that set altruistic goals and objectives and focus on consensus building, education, and mutual understanding as strategies to improve human relations. This approach seeks to reduce prejudice and conflict through understanding, cultural exchange, conflict resolution, communication, and dialogue. It subscribes to the pluralistic notion of "we are the same because we all are human beings." Dawes (1980) discussed an altruistic motivation as crucial to eliciting cooperation between individuals and groups, pointing out that a central social dilemma facing individuals and groups is that individual altruism can often be realized only by cooperating with the collective.

The Black/Korean Alliance (BKA) and the Latino/Black Roundtable (LBR) were created with the abstract goal of improving relations between communities with varying histories of intergroup tensions. The premise of these coalitions relied heavily on the altruistic motivation of coalition members and on their ability to transform a highly abstract goal into concrete action. The coalition members' altruistic motivation could be realized only if the Korean American, African American, and Latino communities joined in the coalition's goals and activities. Individuals who decided to participate in the BKA and LBR believed that improving intergroup communication and understanding would reduce intergroup tension. To a certain extent, the BKA and LBR were able to move their dialogue into joint action, but dialogue and cross-cultural communication were not enough to build interethnic unity.

The human relations approach has been criticized as being elitist. Coalitions focusing on improving relations between different cultural groups have the daunting task of making communities want to work together. One of the major shortcoming of altruistic coalition approach is that it focuses too much on why coalitions form and too little how they are maintained over time. That is, the reasons that people join a coalition are not necessarily the same reasons that they decide to stay or leave.

The Interest-Based Approach

Carmichael and Hamilton (1967), who provided the ideological impetus for the black power movement of the 1960s, advocated interest-based coalitions. Specifically, they advanced a cultural nationalist ideology that politicized racial pride and self-determination and argued against altruistic coalitions with white liberals, which had played a dominant role in the civil rights movement during the 1950s and 1960s. Carmichael and Hamilton contended that blacks should mobilize their own community and promote black pride and self-determination before seeking to form coalitions with others. They proposed four conditions for a viable coalition: (1) the recognition by the participating parties of their respective self-interests, (2) the mutual belief that each party stands to achieve their goals by joining the coalition, (3) the recognition that each party must make decisions based on forces outside itself, and (4) the realization that the coalition has specific and identifiable, as opposed to general and vague, goals. Once the groups meet these conditions, they can coalesce around their shared interests. The interest-based approach, therefore, emphasizes race and racial oppression as the most salient features of political identity.

Interest-based coalitions are often difficult to maintain. For instance, what happens if one or more coalition members no longer feel that their interests are being served by participating in the coalition? Interest-based coalitions assume that members will participate only if they perceive potential benefits, so if one member of a coalition is interested in promoting only its own self-interest, the coalition may not be able to accommodate it. For example, the pressure to protect the self-interests of their own communities contributed to the demise of the BKA and the LBR in the early 1990s (Diaz-Veizades and Chang 1996).

Coalition building requires sacrifice from and accommodation to the participating individual and/or group members, so interest-based coalitions often break up when participants compete with one another in pursuing their own self-interests. Coalition also is not possible without "trust" among the members. As we shall demonstrate later, the members of the BKA and the LBR could not get beyond narrow nationalism and racial group loyalties because they pursued their own self-interests (Regalado 1995, p. 46). Furthermore, interest-based coalitions based on race can succeed only if other conflicting interests (class and gender) can be overcome, de-emphasized, resolved, or ignored altogether.

The Issue-Based Approach

During the 1990s, the sudden influx of low-income refugees and immigrants into the most economically depressed neighborhoods and communities of Los Angeles posed new challenges to the city's coalition-building process. An African American police officer's beating a Latino youth led to a conflict between the Latino and African American communities in Compton (a city in Los Angeles County). Clashes between Latino immigrants and African American communities have been also reported in other parts of the United States. In East Palo Alto, California, a decade ago, 85 percent of the student population were black, but today almost 70 percent of the 5,000 students are Latino. The five-person school board, however, has just one Latino member (Ratnesar 1997, p. 52). Grassroots-organizing models could be the best strategy for Latinos and African Americans to meet the needs of both communities (MCC 1996, p. 41). In the past, African Americans struggled against white supremacy and institutional discrimination, but today Latinos confront institutions headed by African American leaders and politicians. Thus Latinos are demanding equal representation while African Americans are trying to hold onto the power they gained during the 1960s. In the 1990s, therefore, we are faced with the new question of how to reconcile the Latinos' demand for equal representation and the African Americans' feeling of displacement.

Issue-based coalitions have been proposed as an alternative model for resolving interminority conflicts, as the issue-based coalition model recognizes that dialogue and cross-cultural communication alone are not enough to build interethnic cooperation. Whereas altruistic coalitions often lack specific goals and objectives, neighborhood coalitions based on concrete issues seem more likely to be able to transcend race and ethnicity. For example, such coalitions have effectively mobilized residents around issues of improving sanitation services, creating better community-police relations, securing capital for economic development, improving school resources, and developing education curricula. In Los Angeles, several issue-based and neighborhood-based coalitions have been successful: the Southern California Organizing Committee (SCOC), United Neighborhood Organizations (UNO), and Watts/Century Latino Organization (WCLO). These groups represent the kind of grassroots activity that is increasing and becoming more effective in Los Angeles, as they have effectively reduced intergroup tension and mobilized local residents to work collectively toward social and economic justice (see MCC 1996, p. 19).[1] Despite these successes, however, many questions about the viability of multiracial coalitions have yet to be answered.

Multiple-Identity Politics as a Basis for Coalitions

Skeptics of biracial or multiracial coalitions point out the inability of race-based coalitions to recognize other structural factors (class and gender) that can undermine broad racial alliances. An overemphasis on race and/or racial differences can increase the division and separation of different ethnic and racial groups. Multiple-identity politics, therefore, rejects racial essentialism and recognizes "differential disempowerment" among the various communities (J. Chang 1994). In other words, other identities—such as gender, class, sexual orientation, and religious affiliation—also are critical (Collins 1993, Crenshaw 1989, Gitlin 1993b, Morris and Mueller 1992). Multiple-identity politics rejects the cultural nationalist politics of "racial identity" as the only salient basis for social and political mobilization (see Chung 1995). Rather than overemphasizing racial identity as the best basis for social and political mobilization, it recognizes the multidimensional nature of oppression. Accordingly, building a coalition around interests besides race is not only possible but also necessary in the struggle to overcome all aspects of domination. For example, the Third World Liberation Front (TWLF) of the 1960s cut across racial boundaries and successfully incorporated African Americans, Latinos, Asian Americans, and Native Americans into a cultural and political movement that demanded racial equality and social justice. The TWLF embraced the term *people of color* to construct a political consciousness among nonwhites of different ethnicities who suffered from economic exploitation, political subjugation, and racial oppression in America.

The construction of a broad political consciousness is necessary because communities of color have become more stratified during the past two decades. Multiple-identity politics, therefore, can recognize and reconcile shared and conflicting interests to minimize differences and solidify commonalties to enhance coalition building among and between groups.

Despite the prevalence of coalitions in both the labor and political spheres (Brecher and Costello 1990, Omatsu 1995, Sonenshein 1993), there has been relatively little research on cross-cultural community coalitions (although see Henry 1980, Oliver and Johnson 1984, Regalado 1995, Uhlaner 1991). The creation of cross-cultural alliances and coalitions may very well be an important step in reducing the cultural and ideological fragmentation found in many urban centers around the globe. Indeed, the future of urban politics and community planning may lie not in monolithic coalitions but, rather, in issue-oriented coalitions, which wax and wane (Oliver and Grant 1995). As Regalado (1995) indicated, the time is ripe for fashioning new and innovative coalitions that can meet the needs of marginalized communities that are experiencing economic and demographic changes and the consequent intracommunity fragmentation. The Black-Korean Alliance (BKA) and the Latino-Black Roundtable (LBR) were intended to address these needs, so we next shall look at their development and dissolution.

The Creation of the BKA and the LBR

In response to the tensions and conflicts described in chapter 2, the Los Angeles Human Relations Commission (LAHRC) established the BKA in 1983 and the LBR in 1986. The LAHRC was established by an ordinance of the Los Angeles Board of Supervisors and is dedicated to promoting educational activities that raise public awareness of human relations issues. Both coalitions were started as independent interventions reflecting the concerns of individual LAHRC staff at the time, rather than as part of an overarching human relations plan for the city.

The BKA was started in response to specific complaints by African Americans and Korean Americans regarding customer-merchant interactions. During the first few years of its existence (1983–1986), the BKA did little, since aside from these initial complaints, there were no other visible signs of tension between Korean Americans and African Americans. But this changed in 1986 when the murder of four Korean merchants propelled the BKA into action. In response, the BKA focused on disseminating positive information about Korean American–African American relations and taking measures to prevent further outbreaks of violence that could be construed as having racial implications.

The LBR was originally conceived as a community organization specifically focused on the Watts area's King-Drew Medical Center. Tensions had arisen over African American concerns that Latinos were taking over an important community resource and also over Latino concerns that the few Latinos employed by the center undermined its ability to service their expanding constituency (Oliver and Johnson 1984). According to one of the LAHRC staff responsible for initiating the LBR, the idea for an issues-based alliance was not supported by city officials, who felt that the sensitivity of the King-Drew issue would bring to the surface the deeper issue of African American–Latino political control in the area. The LBR was therefore started with the more general goal of strengthening the relationship between African Americans and Latinos and improving the quality of life and sense of well-being for both groups.

Organizational Structure. To ensure cross-cultural representation, both the BKA and the LBR had rotating cochairs. The BKA's primary structure was provided by five task forces: employment, community education and cultural exchange, fund-raising, religious leadership, and economic development. The LBR's members spent much of their time drawing up requirements for membership and a mission statement.

For both coalitions, the role of the LAHRC staff was limited to coordinating the groups' initial formulation. In addition, the LAHRC staff were responsible for recording the meetings' minutes and reporting the coalitions' activities to the LAHRC board. Maintaining the coalitions was the responsibility of the cochairs.

Membership. Members of the BKA and LBR were persons chosen by the LAHRC staff. The LBR membership represented community, educational, and business interests, drawing members from the Los Angeles NAACP, Mexican American Legal Defense and Education Fund (MALDEF), Los Angeles Urban League, East Los Angeles Community Union, Black Employees Association, Los Angeles Chicano Employees Association, Southern California Gas Company, Pacific Bell, Los Angeles Mayor's Office, and Los Angeles Unified School District (LAUSD).

The BKA members represented a broader spectrum of persons from church and community organizations, reflecting the fact that a black-Korean church organization had been established before the BKA was formed. The BKA's membership also included persons from the United Way, Korean American Grocery Association of Southern California, Westminster Neighborhood Association, Korean Small Business Association of South Los Angeles, Los Angeles Urban League, Southern Christian Leadership Conference, and several other community organizations.

Coalition Events

Latino-Black Roundtable. One of the first events sponsored by the LBR was an all-day seminar on educational issues such as classroom overcrowding, literacy, and student achievement and retention. The objectives were to identify educational models for black and Latino students and to support ongoing efforts to improve the education of black and Latino students. Other projects included an evaluation of the Los Angeles Unified School District's affirmative action program, information forums on youth at risk, redistricting in Los Angeles, voter registration, and the use of force by the Los Angeles Police Department in connection with the beating of Rodney King. The LBR also conducted a career model program at a black college in the area. At the group meetings, members of the LBR discussed the Persian Gulf War, police brutality, conflict resolution, human relations training, multiculturalism, and gang violence. The general sentiment of the LBR members we interviewed was that although they had learned a great deal from the meetings, they were not always able to translate this knowledge into action.

Black-Korean Alliance. In 1986, the Community Education and Cultural Exchange subcommittee of the BKA sponsored the Christmas Food-Basket Giveaway, a program that was discontinued after 1987 because of the poor reception of the African American community. In 1987, the same subcommittee also sponsored cultural awareness, crime prevention, and small business seminars. The religious subcommittee arranged pulpit exchanges between the communities and participated in exchange programs that sponsored African American youths on trips to South Korea.

A central activity of the BKA was developing a "code of ethics" for Korean American merchants, which suggested how they should interact with their customers (e.g., smile at the customer, place change in the customer's hands rather than on the counter). These suggestions were printed on placards to be hung in Korean American–owned stores as a sign of the owner's goodwill. The riots of 1992 and the eventual breakup of the BKA, however, prevented the distribution of the placards.

The Coalitions' Dissolution

During the LBR's first years, the number of active members fluctuated between twenty to thirty, but by early 1992, this number had dropped to an average of fewer than ten active participants. Despite efforts by the cochairs and the LAHRC staff to revive the members' interest (e.g., distributing a survey to identify coalition concerns, holding a workshop on conflict resolution training), attendance at meetings did not improve. In March 1992, when only two members came to a meeting to discuss the LBR's future, the cochairs decided to disband the organization, recommending that the LAHRC develop alternative strategies to improve black-Latino relations.

By the end of the 1980s, the BKA's meetings and coalition functions were likewise poorly attended. The BKA's remaining active members made a concerted effort over a one-year period (1991/92) to maintain the coalition (Doherty 1992), and in January 1992, they held a daylong workshop/mediation session to come up with a way in which the alliance could continue to function. Although there were only about ten active BKA members left at the time, the session was very well attended, and a consensus reached was that members would try to revitalize the BKA by recruiting new members and sponsoring events. But before they were able to act on these ideas, the events of April 1992 intervened. Because the BKA was already weakened, it was not able to withstand the increase in tensions between the communities after the riots. Consequently, the BKA was officially disbanded in November 1992, although by April it already had really ceased to exist.

The Reasons for the LBR's and the BKA's Dissolution

The reasons for the LBR's and the BKA's breakup were a combination of the structure of the coalitions themselves (e.g., their membership), the nature of the larger communities involved, and the assumptions underlying their formation in the first place.

Resources. A common problem continually voiced by both LBR and BKA members was the lack of human and financial resources—the lack of paid staffing was perhaps the resource missed most. Although the LAHRC provided two paid staff members, the commission itself was pitifully understaffed, and those staff members assigned to the coalitions could not give them adequate time and resources. The coalition members were already overextended with personal and professional commitments, and without staff to oversee their work, it was easy for members to accept tasks but never finish them.

To many LBR and BKA members, this lack of resources symbolized the fact that human relations were not a priority of the city administration. They repeatedly observed that if the city were truly concerned with improving community race relations, the mayor's office would have given groups such as the BKA and LBR much higher priority. As it was, the most attention the mayor's office paid to the coalitions was two breakfast meetings held with the BKA in 1986 and assistance in mediating the John's Market boycott in 1991.

The lack of financial resources could have been partially addressed through membership dues, something that neither coalition considered. Dues also would have given the members a tangible commitment to make the organization succeed, but without such a commitment, the members lost interest.

Membership. For the BKA and LBR to achieve their goal of improving community relations, their members had to be able to develop a wide base of community support. Were they able to gain the community's trust? Did they know the communities well enough to understand their needs and preferences? Were they able to deliver a sizable constituency when necessary? Two factors impeded the members' ability to meet these demands: (1) the structure of the membership, which was made up of individual rather than organizational members, and (2) the class differences between the members and the communities they served.

To make the coalition's membership as inclusive as possible, each coalition was composed of individuals rather than organizations (i.e., a member of the LBR who also was a member of MALDEF would not officially represent MALDEF in coalition meetings or functions). Without the long history of community involvement that many organizations enjoyed, individual members did have an extensive constituency base to draw on. In addition, the meetings and events of both the BKA and the LBR were poorly attended, a problem that might have been avoided had the events been publicized and supported by organizations that were well known either locally or nationally.

The use of individual versus organizational membership also allowed members to use the coalitions for individual gain. A common theme we heard in our interviews with both BKA and LBR members was that some people had joined the group in order to advance personal or political goals. An African American member of the BKA stated,

> I think that there were some people [Koreans] there who were only there because they wanted to stabilize the situation so they could stay in business so they could make big money and run their businesses. . . . We also had, I suspect, a few people . . . who were regular members of the BKA who were

black business people, and primarily in it to get some more for themselves. [We] didn't have enough people who were sincere to minimize the effects of those kinds of people.

Some members also suspected that others joined the coalition in order to elevate their name and face recognition, since both groups, but particularly the BKA, were often represented in the media.

Some African American members of the BKA felt that Korean Americans were interested only in improving black-Korean relations as a means of improving the area's business climate and thereby improving their source of revenue. In turn, some Korean American members believed that some African American members were interested only in removing Korean American–owned businesses from African American neighborhoods. Not knowing exactly why a person joined the coalition encouraged speculation about individual motivation and made building a base of trust extremely difficult.

The membership of both coalitions changed in accordance with individual needs, so time and momentum were wasted as new members learned the coalition's history and goals. As one LBR member told us,

When we have individual [members], they rotate and we don't have a degree of permanency. Whereas if you move it up to the next level and you have the organizations that represent the individuals, then you get some level of stability. So that's the first thing, and so there might be politics, but it's tied into a recognized . . . legitimate organization. And those organizations then tie in to some political strategy. But we didn't do that . . . we specifically, said "individuals and not organizations" . . . that's a real tough sell because individuals rotate.

Members' altruistic motivations were not always able to overcome the competing demands of personal and professional commitments.

For the most part, the coalitions were made up of middle- to upperclass professionals who, though identified as Latino, African American, or Korean American, did not represent the working class or unemployed constituents of their respective communities. In the words of one BKA member,

I'm fading myself out of the whole thing because it became very, very disgusting. Because they wouldn't listen . . . you see, experience is the best school master, and longevity is the best teacher You see, I don't want anybody who just came on the scene, somebody fresh out of the ACLU [American Civil Liberties Union], USC [University of Southern California],

Berkeley [University of California], or Davis [University of California] uh uh . . . they don't understand the basic problem, what the needs are.

Later in the interview he added, "The government has never been able to solve our problems, the problems of the black people . . . it's always from the middle class up. They never come to Watts, they only come to Watts when there is a crisis." Members who were middle-class professionals also were not accountable to the communities that the coalitions were designed to serve. That is, these members could make decisions and sponsor events without having to justify their decision to any constituency other than the affiliate organization to which they belonged. A BKA member recalled,

> There were times when we were talking about the customer/merchant code of ethics and we had no merchants; we were negotiating a code of conduct . . . and the people that had to live and abide by it were not at the table. Or the customer that is going to go to that corner market is not there to say "this is what I want."

Problems were created in the BKA because the membership did not sufficiently reflect the established leadership of the Korean American community. One Korean member observed,

> We were dealing with only one segment of the Korean community and that was the young people, and those traditional Koreans in Koreatown we never knew or never saw, and they're the leaders. The old people are the leaders of the community. The young people don't lead that community. They have leadership positions, but they don't necessarily lead the community.

According to another member,

> On the Korean-American side, there were generational, issues . . . people like me who were the younger folks, the diehards who stuck to the end speak to the distancing of community . . . we couldn't deliver on the Korean American grocers, and those were the people who needed to be [there], who were key to all [of this].

The LBR had no representatives from the newer immigrant community, an oversight that was due partly to the absence of ties between the established Mexican American community and the more recently arrived Mexican and Central American immigrants (Hayes-Bautista 1993, Ramos 1993). It was not until the 1992 riots that many Latino leaders discovered vast segments of the Los Angeles Latino community (mainly the newest immigrants) that had been completely ignored by the existing Latino leadership. Ruben Martinez criticized the leadership of the established Mexican American community for being "virtually silent, unwilling or unable to deal with the Salvadoran problem in Pico-Union" (Institute for Alternative Journalism 1992, p. 33). Ironically, many of the issues that the LBR sought to address were directly related to black-Latino relations in the context of the most recent wave of Latino immigration.

Contending parties can come to an agreement more easily if they have equal power, be it economic or political (Stolte 1990). But this was not the case in either the BKA or the LBR. The perception by some Korean members of the BKA was that the African American community's political power and skill gave the black members of the coalition the ability to substantially affect community attitudes and dynamics. One Korean American member spoke about the development of the customer-merchant code of ethics:

> I thought that [the code of ethics] was kind of very unfair . . . that just shouldn't be only for the Koreans and it should have been for everybody and they [African Americans] were really targeting Korean merchants and obviously, at the political level, the Koreans had the least power, and when there's a crisis the African American leadership comes out very strong, and that's where the imbalance [comes in]; they're just pinpointing and blaming everything on Koreans instead of looking at the entire infrastructure problem. And I'm saying that you have an African American mayor, you have the city council, you have all these people and the government couldn't do anything about the south central problem, why you expect Koreans to go in there and make a difference . . . that was very unfair.

On the surface, African Americans do appear to hold substantially more political power in Los Angeles than Korean Americans do. From 1968 to 1993, Los Angeles was governed by an African American mayor, and at the time we conducted the interviews for this project, the chief of the Los Angeles Police Department was an African American as well. The city council had three African American representatives, and blacks were prominent on the school board. As in any other larger metropolitan area, however, political power is often subordinate to economic power, and the real power in Los Angeles lies with those with the most property and investment capital (Davis 1992).

Alternatively, African American coalition members felt that since the Korean American community appeared to have an economic advantage, they should have been the ones to take the initiative by forming joint partnerships with African Americans or by hiring African Americans in their businesses. This sentiment reflects a popular misconception, often reinforced by the media, that all Korean Americans are rich. In reality, however, many Korean Americans are barely making ends meet. Moreover, "successful" store ownership often requires twelve-hour workdays, six days a week, using (unpaid) family labor. Similar to Koreans' perceptions of African Americans' political power, African Americans' perceptions of Koreans' economic power demonstrates a lack of understanding of the Korean American community's economic situation.

The balance of power in the LBR between African Americans and Latinos resulted from each community's different emphasis on building cross-community links. Both Latino and African American members stated that when the coalition was formed, human relations were simply not a priority for the Latino community. As one member of the LBR pointed out,

> There was a really strong feeling among the Latino activist civil rights organizations that their thrust needed to be to make everybody get out of their way because it was their time and to just kind of spend time dealing with traditional friends, or even traditional enemies, wasn't their thing. They wanted to increase voter involvement, get their people elected; they wanted to get their people appointed they wanted to be, not just numbers, but for their numbers to reflect their authority in the city.

In essence, the Latino community's potential political strength was such that they could not afford to spend valuable organizational and individual resources on forming an alliance with a group that was politically and economically stronger. The fact that the two groups did not hold intergroup relations in equal importance resulted in an imbalance in African American and Latino membership, with the African American members generally holding more visible and powerful positions in the coalition than the Latino members did. This imbalance in turn made it difficult for the LBR to decide on goals and events that reflected the needs of both communities.

Nationalism and Ethnic Solidarity

Building cross-cultural coalitions essentially means breaking down social, political, and economic barriers between groups. Although breaking down these barriers between small numbers of people may be possible over time, they may be raised again when groups feel threatened or are attacked. Such was the case with the BKA and LBR; the advances made between individual members were not strong enough to withstand the forces of ethnic solidarity and nationalism in the broader communities.

The beginning of the end for the BKA was the Latasha Harlins/Soon Ja Du incident. During this time, relations between African Americans and Korean Americans were polarized as powerful factions within each community voiced increasingly divisive sentiments. A highly visible segment of the African American community joined in a boycott of Soon Ja Du's store, and other segments united to oust the judge responsible for sentencing Mrs. Du. Many Korean Americans, already perceiving their community as being under siege because of the many Korean American merchants victimized by crime, closed ranks behind Mrs. Du. An African American member of the BKA told us: "Koreans had . . . coalitions or whatever type of organization to save their own. I was in the BKA when they were rallying for money for Mrs. Du . . . they were able to get a black attorney that they had to pay over $250,000 . . . and she walked away."[2]

This member's statement reflects a popular misconception that all Korean Americans supported Soon Ja Du and Judge Karlin's ruling, and it was at this time that he left the BKA. In reality, however, Korean Americans were very divided over this issue and did not, in fact, raise $250,000 on behalf of Mrs. Du. What is important is that some African Americans believed that Korean Americans had provided substantial financial assistance for the case, a misperception typical of the misinformation and consequent distance that characterized many coalition interactions. As another member stated,

> I realized that it was a major crisis also for BKA and I was very disappointed that our own members, BKA members, that when we needed their support most, that the support was not available from the African American leaders. I guess that's where we saw our limits there, and I said, "I don't want to get involved anymore."

The Latasha Harlins incident demonstrated the difficulties of developing coalitions of marginalized communities. In a time of crisis, when both communities felt attacked not only by each other but also by the larger system of inequities, the groups invariably drew inward. For African American coalition members to have supported the Korean American community would have been viewed by the larger African American community as a betrayal. It would have hampered the alliance's ability to make inroads in the black community, and the African American coalition members also would have been ostracized by other black leaders. The same could be said about the Korean American coalition members.

The LBR faced similar problems in regard to the issue of bilingual education. As one member described the discussion of bilingual education at an LBR meeting, there was simply silence—a silence attributable to the politically sensitive nature of the topic. In the African American community, bilingual education has been a particularly divisive issue. Some people see it as taking away resources available to teach African American children, and others see bilingual education as providing an opportunity to teach African American children a second language. Consequently, taking a public stance on this issue in the LBR meetings was politically dangerous, since there was no guarantee that a coalition member's views would not be repeated outside the coalition and jeopardize external political alliances that might be needed at a later date. Given the need for disenfranchised communities to band together to achieve even minimal goals, there was a strong need to keep intact those alliances within the community, even though doing so might weaken ties with other racial or cultural groups.

The need to maintain strong ties with the members of one's own cultural community is underscored in a metropolitan area such as Los Angeles where the political and economic climate has historically been marked by competition and tension among different ethnic factions (Sonenshein 1993). Cross-cultural relations in Los Angeles has not yet reached the point that individuals are as willing to trust members of other cultural groups as much as they are willing to trust members of their own.[3]

Cross-Cultural Dynamics

Because the members of the LBR had a common culture and language, as they were, for the most part, established professionals, cross-cultural dynamics were more problematic for the BKA than for the LBR. In the BKA, cross-cultural differences arose mainly because many Korean immigrant members knew little about the process of dialogue and politics in the United States. A BKA member explained,

> In a lot of ways, and maybe this speaks to the state of coalitions in L.A; particularly with new communities, communities of color and immigrant community groups is that, some of us have never been invited to the table; they don't know what it's like to be given a seat at the table and negotiate.

... Not all of us know what to say and what to do, what etiquette means about negotiating at the table. And I think those are the things that often get overlooked. I mean how do you all of a sudden say you've got the power to self-determine, when some folks don't know how to articulate their position, or they don't speak English, when some folks because of their economic background and their history, don't know how these things works, don't know what the dynamics should be.

One African American member we interviewed interpreted the Korean Americans' silence as a sign of their unwillingness to discuss certain issues. But in reality, their silence may simply have indicated that they did not know how to discuss them.

An Analysis of Black-Korean and Black-Latino Relations

Using a Dialogue Model

Both the BKA and the LBR adopted a dialogue approach to intergroup relations, which assumes that intergroup tension can be reduced by improving communication and understanding. The choice of this model was reflected in the events sponsored by the coalitions—seminars, pulpit exchanges, workshops, the black-Korean code of ethics, conferences, and so forth. A BKA member with much experience in community organizing and development explained: A model that focuses on consensus building, education, and mutual understanding is an elitist approach to organizing. She contrasted this approach with an advocacy approach, which brings people together to fight for a common interest, thereby providing a concrete goal around which people's emotions and energies can be rallied.

The crisis level of economic underdevelopment in both the African American and Latino communities (and, to a somewhat lesser extent, the Korean American community) did indeed require direct intervention. One member of the BKA described how when he underscored the urgency of attending to the needs of the African American community, other coalition members told him to be patient, that the process of improving community relations took time. He replied, "We don't have time, we have to move, we got to develop something now, right now. You know these guys out here that are gangbangers, you got to get something for them, because there's another crop that's coming along."

This use of a dialogue model reflects the operating ideology of the Los Angeles Human Relations Commission: facilitating communication and disseminating knowledge. An example from the BKA shows the coalition's inability to address the underlying issues of economic development. At one point, the BKA identified the need for joint African American/Korean American economic development projects, and one African American businessman and one Korean American businessman who were members of the BKA drew up a joint proposal for a bid on janitorial services for the Los Angeles airport. As they became more involved in the project, they realized that what they needed was an extensive lobbying network in city hall, something that the BKA did not have and that the LAHRC staff was not equipped to provide. Thus without the ability to address economic development, their attempt to form an intergroup alliance failed.

The mistake of relying solely on the LAHRC's human relations model also was symbolized by the inability to concentrate the LBR's attention on the King-Drew Medical Center. Because the LAHRC is a governmental organization, it has political constraints, which limit its ability to support any community activity too directly focused on changing the region's existing social or political infrastructure. A model limited to dialogue rather than activism thus partly reflected the LAHRC's political constraints.

Assumptions Regarding African American–Korean and African American–Latino Relations

The formation of the coalitions, the choice of the coalitions' agendas, and the choice of a dialogue model approach all reflect underlying assumptions about the nature of intergroup tension and resolution. A crucial assumption was that the issues were truly between all African Americans and all Korean Americans and between all African Americans and all Latinos. But this assumption overlooked the fact that the Korean American, African American, and Latino communities are highly diverse groups and that the relations between them are really between subgroups of the larger groups rather than between the larger groups. For example, the Korean Immigrant Workers' Advocate (KIWA) staged several protests and boycotts of Korean restaurants in Los Angeles to protect the rights of both Korean and Latino workers. Therefore, problematic relations between African Americans and Korean Americans in Los Angeles are more accurately defined as black-Korean customer-merchant relations in south central Los Angeles than as black-Korean relations in general. Not all Korean Americans are merchants, for example.

Furthermore, the BKA's focus on exclusively black-Korean issues prevented the members from analyzing the customer-merchant relationship in the larger socioeconomic and sociopolitical context of urban underdevelopment in the south central area. Labeling the customer-merchant relationship as "black-Korean tension" also excluded the Latino community of south central Los Angeles from the dialogue. Since black-Korean tensions were inseparable from issues of economic development and since the Latino community is the majority community in south central Los Angeles, the tensions between Korean American merchants and their African American customers could not be resolved without including the Latinos.

The size and diversity of the Latino community made it extremely difficult for the LBR to focus on any one particular aspect of black-Latino relations, because the Latino community is really several different communities, each with its own problems. In Los Angeles, the so-called Latino community is made up of persons of Mexican and Central and Latin American descent; it is made up of seventh-generation Californians as well as people who have only recently arrived, either legally or illegally. There also are economic, political, educational, and religious differences within the Latino community, which are compounded in a city as large as Los Angeles where each geographical area (e.g., Koreatown versus south central) has it own sense of community. The needs of the immigrant Latino community in Koreatown thus may be vastly different from those of the larger Mexican American community in south central Los Angeles. Consequently, the different needs of each of these communities make it difficult to set coalition priorities. One member explained:

> There were too many agendas, so you're too confused. You've got too many things out here; each community has its own priorities. We had many focus meetings where we'd decide these are things we're going to focus on, and then you'd go back three months later and people would say, "Well, no, these are the priorities."

Another member added, "What I'm discovering now . . . is that each community is uniquely different and their priorities are different. Every community has its own multicultural issues. . . . I believe that coalitions like that have to define themselves at the community level and define the issues [at the community level]." The difficulty in defining the LBR's agenda also was a result of various aspects of black-Latino relations. As mentioned earlier, Latino-black relations are not framed primarily by customer-merchant interactions, as are black-Korean relations, but reach across many different institutional and social spaces. According to an LBR member,

> Issues between blacks and Latinos were everywhere, in the school system, between lawyers, in regard to affirmative actions. That was agreed on. [We] couldn't agree on what issues, at what point to intervene, and who could intervene. Several people within the coalition felt that the schools would be an appropriate place to intervene; others, however, felt the focus should be on labor and the representative hiring of Latinos [e.g., at the King-Drew Center].

Without a precipitating event such as the violence erupting in black-Korean relations and without a detailed analysis of the issues facing blacks and Latinos, the "problem" of black-Latino relations became too big and abstract, and as one member said, "You couldn't get your arms around it."

The Dissolution of the BKA and the LBR

Given the relatively new awareness of the need to move coalition building beyond traditional coalition partners and parameters, the formation of the BKA and the LBR was, at the minimum, courageous and far-reaching in its scope and potential. Invariably, the coalition members we interviewed stated that if given the opportunity again, they would still try to build a coalition, although not without making modifications based on past experience. In addition, for many members, their participation in the coalitions resulted in long-standing friendships with people they would not otherwise have met. And for several people, their coalition membership brought them valuable professional contacts that continue to this day to foster the coalitions' goals of developing cross-cultural cooperation.

Perhaps the most important contribution of the BKA and LBR was that they both attempted to institutionalize cross-cultural coalition building. The need for making human relations an integral aspect of modern-day urban planning cannot be underestimated, and all the persons we interviewed agreed on the importance of developing coalitions in the future. In many of our interviews regarding the future direction of building coalitions and improving human relations in Los Angeles, the following themes and suggestions emerged:

1. Coalitions need to develop a strong resource base, by both having dues-paying organizations as members and building the political will to support human relation efforts. In order for the coalitions to remain as inclusive as possible, dues could be set on a sliding scale.
2. Coalitions must be neighborhood based, thereby reflecting neighborhood-specific demographic and economic problems.
3. Coalitions must be issue based, with specific and concrete goals that already have community support, for example, improving sanitation services, developing better community-police relations, securing capital for economic development, improving school resources, and drawing up better educational curricula.

If the focus is to be cross-cultural relations, then support must first be obtained from each community before trying to bring the communities together, for example, holding workshops and seminars in the African American, Korean, and Latino communities in anticipation of an eventual African American/Korean American or African American/Latino alliance. Coalitions should be as inclusive as possible, as community relations involve many different groups, and all must be part of the dialogue.

Summary

Although the research presented in this chapter is mainly descriptive, it nevertheless does have some theoretical implications. The first stems from the observation that for the most part, individuals joined the coalitions out of collectivist rather than solely individualistic motivations. This observation contrasts with theory that individuals join coalitions because membership in such an organization maximizes an individually structured payoff matrix (Adrian and Press 1968, Chertkoff 1975, Gamson 1961, Komorita and Chertkoff 1973, Riker 1962). Although it is true that individuals joined the BKA and LBR in order to maximize individual payoffs, for most members, these payoffs could not be quantified in solely individualistic terms, for they were collectivist in nature and related to the desire to advance group-based needs. If anything, for many BKA and

LBR members, coalition membership often resulted in negative payoffs in terms of the amount of time spent and the potential of being alienated from one's community. The greater relative importance of group versus individual need most likely characterizes those coalitions in which the cultural groups represented hold more collectivist/ interdependent value systems than individualistic/independent value systems.

The importance of the external environment also is relevant to understanding the coalition's internal coalition. For example, the coalition's dynamics often were influenced by members' needs to maintain alliances with their respective communities, which did not necessarily support the formalization of cross-community relationships. Similarly, the dynamics between coalition members were directly related to events taking place independently of the coalitions, as in the case of the BKA and the Latasha Harlins/Soon Ja Du situation and in the case of the LBR and the intra- and intercommunity tension surrounding bilingual education. The link between the behavior of individual coalition members and the events occurring in the larger society undoubtedly influence any coalition developed in a fluctuating social, economic, and political context.

One other point we wish to highlight is the uniqueness of cross-cultural coalitions. Central to the dynamics of the BKA and LBR coalitions are the different group-based histories that the coalition members bring with them. In the BKA and LBR, these collective histories included different experiences of oppression, discrimination, and cultural norms and expectations, all of which resulted in differences in the coalition members' goals, for example, the Latino community's need to advance politically even at the expense of developing cross-cultural alliances. The influence of the groups' histories on the coalition's dynamics will be germane when entering coalitions with historically disenfranchised groups whose collective history of betrayal and oppression will influence perceptions of, and behavior toward, other coalition partners.

6

Conflict Resolution and Community Development in Multicultural Urban Centers

Thus far, we have described race relations in Los Angeles from sociological, economic, and psychological perspectives, so we devote this final chapter to a prescription for conflict resolution and community development approaches in multicultural urban centers.

One approach to building communities is to find working models or paradigms that provide human relations experts and community development people with frameworks to guide their actions. Currently, human relations models are separate from community development models, with the former addressing traditional human relations concerns such as reducing prejudice, preventing violence and hate crimes, and resolving disputes, and the latter addressing issues such as affordable housing and small-business loans. Attending only to a conflict's human relations and psychological dimensions (e.g., stereotypes, prejudice, communication) fails to address some of the conflict's root causes (e.g., lack of job opportunities).

At the same time, since defining and achieving development goals in multicultural areas require the cooperation of different ethnic and class groups, the conflict's psychological elements must be considered along with the development concerns. Thus what we really are calling for is an expanded notion of conflict resolution that combines conflict resolution with social change, community development, and community organizing; that is, human relations approaches must be developed in conjunction with community development approaches.

The challenge of this approach is that it requires a fundamental rethinking of current conflict resolution practices. In a comprehensive report of the status of human relations work in Los Angeles, the Multi-cultural Collaborative (1996) concluded the following:

1. Institutional responses to human and race relations are fragmented and driven by crisis.
2. Current dispute resolution strategies focus on one-on-one conflicts rather than intergroup and community conflicts.
3. Public- and private-sector planning for economic development and resource allocation typically pays little or no attention to its impact on human relations and racial conflict.
4. School-based human relations projects and curriculum usually focus on cultural appreciation and diversity, rarely attempting to teach the awareness and skills that students need to understand and deal with the causes of intergroup conflict.
5. Human relations training that mainly targets managers and employees of public and private institutions concentrates on cultural appreciation and diversity rather than economic development and social change.
6. Aside from the alliances that promote more diversity in the media workplace, few efforts try to find ways to enhance the mainstream media's coverage of positive intergroup relations.
7. Previous intergroup collaboration efforts have been limited in scope and centered on dialogue.
8. The greater Los Angeles area lacks sustainable mechanisms for training and supporting grassroots leaders in effective interethnic community–organizing efforts.
9. At a time when Los Angeles's diverse communities most need to work together to address institutional causes of poverty and tension, the city's leadership is becoming more polarized.

These nine criticisms of current human relations efforts are reflected in the MCC's belief that the most promising means of reducing intergroup tension is to support grassroots community-organizing efforts and, in this way, encourage diverse groups to work together to achieve social and economic justice. The MCC's conclusions about current human relations approaches underscore the need to link conflict resolution approaches to community development concerns.

Alternative Dispute Resolution

The conflict resolution paradigm labeled *alternative dispute resolution* (ADR) is alternative in that it is an alternative to the traditional method of resolving conflict through the court system. In response to over-crowded court schedules, mediation has been increasingly mandated as the first step in resolving conflicts. As discussed by Adler (1993), the ADR "movement" has developed more as a reaction to the legal system's need to relieve the courts than as a response to the dynamics and structure of community-based conflicts. Essentially, replacing the court-based ap-proach to conflict resolution with an alternative-dispute approach has shifted the concern from achieving justice to maintaining harmonious relations. As Nader (1993) pointed out, community-based mediation, whether practiced in Los Angeles or elsewhere, is based on the underlying belief that disputes are the consequences of people not acting as they should.

Mediation, however, recognizes that conflict arises primarily as a result of perceived differences in interest and miscommunication. Conse-quently, the best means of resolving conflicts is for the parties (the indi-viduals or groups in dispute) to gain a greater understanding of each other's perspectives. The knowledge that one party gains about the other decreases the chances of future disputes (Hill 1995). Mediation and "medarb" (a combination of mediation and arbitration) therefore pro-vide the means by which disputing parties can begin to understand the perspective of the other as well as discuss conflicting issues with a neutral third party who can redirect and rephrase communication toward a con-structive outcome. Mediation therefore concentrates as much on com-munication as on settlement.

A mediation session that follows the mediation model most often used in the United States generally proceeds as follows: The dispute is brought to the attention of a community mediation center by one of the disputing parties. The mediation center then contacts the other party and, usually through a series of phone calls, sets up a time and place where the two (or more) parties can come together with a mediator or a mediation team. In an interethnic dispute, the mediation center tries to gather a team of me-diators representing the ethnicity of the conflicting parties. When the parties meet, each is given an opportunity to describe the conflict from its own perspective. The mediators then tell the parties what the central is-sues in the dispute appear to be. The parties discuss each issue with the assistance of the mediators. The principal function of the mediators is to facilitate constructive communication between the parties, and the goal of the mediation session is to help the parties reach a mutually satisfactory agreement.

At a typical mediation-training session, interested individuals gather, usually for about forty hours. During the training, prospective mediators are taught the fundamentals of good communication (e.g., active listening skills), establishing the framework of a basic mediation, dealing with parties reluctant to reach an agreement, helping parties define the central issues in dispute, writing up an agreement, and learning the legal ramifications of mediation. Once the mediators complete their training, they usually join a private mediation practice or volunteer at a community mediation organization from which they are sent to wherever they are needed. Volunteer mediators address landlord-tenant disputes, neighbor-neighbor conflicts, day laborer–resident conflicts, and so forth. In Los Angeles, the practice of sending mediators as "troubleshooters" has often led to situations in which even trained mediators have been unable to obtain the confidence of the parties involved simply because of the perception that "mediation" is alien to the community.

As is clear from this brief description of the mediation process, the conflict resolution model separates disputes from the broader context in which they occur. Linking the presenting dispute to larger political and economic concerns is complicated by the fact that the paradigm requires that the mediator remain neutral rather than take a particular position. Therefore, the mediator cannot point out that a customer-merchant dispute may be related less to ethnic differences between the parties and more to the history of underdevelopment in a particular community or the profit-making concerns of corporate stakeholders in the liquor industry who remain invisible to the parties concerned. The problem in Los Angeles has been that if community mediation organizations are associated with issues such as community development (which almost by definition requires a reallocation of resources and power), certain parties, such as corporate stakeholders, will not develop the trust in the mediation process needed to bring them to the table. Conversely, ignoring the larger issues of community justice makes the mediation process less successful when the long-term resolution of disputes requires changes in basic structures and processes. An advocacy approach means that mediators must address issues of power imbalance (such as those mentioned by some members of the BKA) and ensure that the presenting disputes are linked to the larger process of community development.

In Los Angeles, several attempts have been made to mediate conflicts between Korean American stores owners and their African American customers. The presence of community mediation centers such as the Martin Luther King Dispute Resolution Center and the Asian Pacific Dispute Resolution Center provide a strong base for community mediation efforts. Through their partnership with each other, these two organizations have been able to address the two groups' language and cultural differences by creating mediation teams composed of both African American and Korean American mediators, preferably people from the neighborhoods where the disputing parties work and do business. No matter how successful a mediation is in this situation, however, the resolution of the dispute within the confines of the mediation model does not allow the disputes as experienced by the two parties to be linked to the dispute as rooted in the larger socioeconomic history and present-day context of south central Los Angeles, as discussed in chapter 2. Relying solely on a mediation approach has therefore caused some community mediators to feel as though they are continually putting out a fire without discovering the cause of the blaze.

The mediation model was not, of course, designed to cope with a conflict's structural causes, and furthermore, mediation can serve an important community-building function to the extent that it can teach communication skills and generate goodwill among the parties. According to Bush and Folger (1994), the concept of transformative mediation is a process in which the parties themselves are transformed through the mediation process. The crucial component, however, is linking individual transformation to social and community transformation.

Such a connection requires mediators to abandon their neutrality and belief that they should not be tied to outcomes in order for them to becomes advocates of a democratic process and a just outcome. A commitment to a democratic process requires them to accord equal power to the conflicting parties and to provide a space where each party is given equal time to promote his or her position. When working with immigrant communities, this may mean educating the parties about their rights in the United States. A commitment to a just outcome may require the mediators to recommend a particular position and to educate the parties about the larger economic and political concerns. Commitment to a just outcome may require mediators to "turn the mediation model on its head" by starting first with a common vision for, as an example, customer-merchant relations and then working backward from there.

Linking mediation to structural concerns is not beyond the model's theoretical purview. For example, in his presentation of the mediation process, Moore (1996) listed, among the possible causes of conflict, structural conflict caused partly by the unequal control, ownership, or distribution of resources, as well as unequal power and authority. We cannot say, however, that such issues underlie the conflict and then stop there. If we, as conflict resolution practitioners, are serious about finding the causes of the conflicts described in this book, we must look at the larger issues of structural inequality. Once again referring to the MCC report, our efforts to improve intergroup relations must be linked to social justice, to which we turn next.

Building Collaborative Communities

The neighborhoods we have discussed clearly fit the definition of distressed communities—communities experiencing many problems (e.g., violence, crime, drugs, unemployment and underemployment, teen pregnancy, domestic violence, inadequate housing, deficient transportation, limited health care). In the past, these neighborhoods have relied on federal assistance programs to support community development efforts. Unfortunately, less federal funding is now available for community-based initiatives, and in California, anti-immigrant sentiment has made it very difficult, if not impossible, for immigrant-based community organizations to obtain federal funding to serve the needs of immigrant residents. It therefore is paramount that cities and communities develop proactive approaches that rely less on federal funding and more on the development of coalitions and networks of community members.

What makes this strategy difficult is that distressed communities often lack social capital—the attitudinal, behavioral, and communal glue that holds society together and encompasses relationships among individuals, families, and organizations. The lack of social capital is a particular problem in communities fragmented by racial, ethnic, and class differences, and immigrant communities face the additional challenge of being composed of very mobile populations.

Although the Korean American and Central American communities have a remarkable network of community organizations, these organizations are often ethnic-specific providers without the aim of building cross-cultural coalitions and partnerships. An unfortunate result is that community organizations often find themselves competing for similar funding for programs designed to meet similar needs. Groups such as the Multicultural Collaborative serve the important function of bringing community groups together that may not otherwise do so. By creating social capital—the communication network that binds a community together—communities can begin to create a common vision of development in order to address concerns such as street violence and day care needs.

The idea of rebuilding social capital is implicit in the concept of building collaborative communities, or civic collaboration. The process of civic collaboration is one of problem solving in which all members who have a stake in a community try to resolve problems and create a collaborative vision for their community. To build collaborative communities, schools, community organizations, churches, federal agencies such as the Department of Housing and Urban Development, county and state human relations commissions, community police organizations, local universities and community colleges, and local and state politicians all must work toward a common cause. The Saamspan model from South Africa, to which we now turn, is an example of building community collaboration from a base of racial and ethnic conflict and fragmentation.

Conflict Resolution and Community Building:
The South African Context

Today, racial conflict in South Africa, much like racial conflict in the United States, continues to be intertwined with resource allocation, be it housing, schooling, jobs, land, or diamond mines. What makes the situation of South Africa a good comparison is that the interethnic conflict there encompasses not only the more visible problems of black-white relations but also the increasingly conflictual and tense relations between English- and Afrikaans-speaking people and between "coloreds" (i.e., mixed race) and blacks in different sections of the colored community, and among races as well as ancient castes (such as the Indian communities). Much like Los Angeles, resolving conflicts in South Africa must

simultaneously address both community development and conflict resolution, understanding that communities can develop only when they
have a shared vision of community (Kraybill 1995, Prillaid 1995). South
African conflict resolution practitioners have been forced by the crisis of
economic underdevelopment to create conflict resolution models that
specifically address the confluence of racial conflict and economic disparity. Accordingly, conflict resolution specialists at the Centre for Conflict
Resolution at the University of the Western Cape have developed a training model called Saamspan, an Afrikaans word meaning "to cooperate,"
which implies teamwork and joint efforts in a daunting task (Odendaal
and Spies 1995).

The Saamspan model is based on the assumption not only that development must be linked to community vision but also that conflict results
when fundamental human needs are not met. Conflict resolution therefore becomes the process by which community development is defined as
the ability to meet fundamental human needs such as security, acceptance protection, affection, understanding, participation, creation, identity, and freedom (Odendaal and Spies 1995). Understanding conflict as
arising from the unfulfillment of human needs clearly departs from the
mediation model, which sees conflict as originating in misperception and
miscommunication.

In contrast to the training model just described, which focuses on
teaching communication skills and the structure of the mediation model,
Saamspan training consists of teaching the basics of mediation and also
the reduction of prejudice, learning how to analyze the sources of conflict
(e.g., poverty and the gap between rich and poor), training leaders (e.g.,
group facilitation skills), and learning how to obtain social and capital resources. A central component of each training meeting is a discussion of
the meaning of conflict resolution in a particular community. In addition, each team member chooses an area of specialization, for example,
crisis intervention, conflict in education, policing and dealing with crime,
interpersonal conflict and violence in the family, and community and
economic development. The result is a local team of conflict resolution
experts who are able to address the various needs of their community.
This model serves to empower communities to satisfy their own community relations needs, as opposed to the mediation model in which outside
experts are brought in to fulfill the community's needs.

An important component of the Saamspan training is the inclusion of
all the relevant stakeholders of a community—youth, the elderly, union

leaders, farmers, landowners, educators, and so on. This is particularly important from a community development perspective, since the obstacles to creating a community vision often do not come from those sitting at the table but from those not sitting at the table. In Grabouw, a rural town where a project Saampsan team has been trained, it took approximately six months to put a team in place who would then undergo a two-year training process. At the end of these two years, however, Project Saamspan was able to put together a ten-member Saamspan team reflecting a broad mix of language, age, ethnicity, and class. The team is now actively involved in resolving disputes and designing peace-building processes. Most recently, Grabouw's Saamspan team conducted a community survey to find out peoples' attitudes toward reconciliation—who needs to be reconciled, what stands in the way of intergroup reconciliation, and whether reconciliation is even possible.

Although the Saamspan training contains a community-organizing component, at the same time it is different from the community-organizing models traditionally used in the United States (e.g., the Alinsky models). The central difference is the extent to which the Saamspan model places community organizing in a collaborative context by seeking to include all stakeholders in the training. This differs from the Alinsky models, which place disenfranchised communities in direct confrontation with other community stakeholders such as corporate landowners. Instead, the Saamspan model is based on the belief that for community development to be sustainable, all stakeholders must be part of the problem-solving process.

The Saamspan approach might not be able to be used in communities in Los Angeles, any more than the North American mediation model could be used in those communities for which it was not originally designed. Rather, the Saamspan model provides an interesting way of creating paradigms of community intervention that really are hybrids of many other models, much like many neighborhoods of today are becoming hybrids (or amalgamations) of many different cultural perspectives and lifestyles. The Saamspan model exemplifies Nader's belief (1993) that conflict resolution should not concentrate solely on microprevention (persuading those neighbors to engage in conversation who might otherwise want to kill each other) but macrovention, a process in which conflict resolution practitioners find out "the number and seriousness of disputes occurring in society in order to look for some kind of structural, organization, or productive means of preventing those disputes" (Nader

1993, p. 448). That is, the Saamspan model permits conflict resolution practitioners to educate communities about the causes of community underdevelopment and disenfranchisement.

Application to Los Angeles

The role of economics in the creation of interethnic conflict in Los Angeles links together the different facets of the conflicts we have examined in this book. These conflicts have arisen not so much because of the cultural differences among groups, such as language or lifestyle (although they have certainly exacerbated the hostile relations), but more because of the way in which ethnicity is linked to particular labor, political, and class relations. The relations between African Americans and Korean Americans as described in chapter 2 is a good example of how cross-cultural conflict pertains not only to differences in language but also to the specific economic roles of different cultural groups in the continuing creation and maintenance of an economic system. Relations between Koreans and Latinos are a bit more complex. Here, culture influences intergroup relations (i.e., their different perceptions of the role of street vendors), and the economic and political climate of both these groups may give rise to, if not conflictual, then to somewhat tense and uncertain community relations.

When we include the economic and political aspects of interethnic conflict, the process of conflict resolution suddenly becomes a process of securing capital investment while simultaneously changing the relationship between capital and labor, of bringing hostile parties together in coalition, of building participatory democracy, of providing adequate access to education and health care, of creating employment, of removing weapons from the streets, and of providing opportunities for those people most marginalized by the existing system. All this must be done against the backdrop of ethnic, racial, class, and ideological divisions.

A good example of the need for community-building approaches is the liquor store problem that has divided Koreans and Latinos in the Pico-Union area of Los Angeles (see chapter 4). At the heart of the problem are restrictive zoning regulations that discourage economic development. Los Angeles's zoning regulations follow the suburban town model, in which land is parceled contiguously and in standard sizes. As discussed by Rodriguez and Vasquez-Rodriguez (1993), the development in Pico-Union has been primarily through conditional-use permits or zoning variances. Los Angeles's restrictive zoning practices include a high percentage of land parcels zoned as residential rather than as commercial, trip-count specifications that do not take into account the fact that the majority of residents do not own automobiles, stringent parking requirements, and so forth. Restrictive zoning regulations have led to vacant parcels of land, oddly shaped parcels, and an inefficient use of space, all of which has resulted in the underutilization of the land and, consequently, the underdevelopment of the area.

Compensating for the overabundance of liquor stores requires more than strengthening the regulations on liquor sales or converting liquor stores into laundromats (a move begun after the civil disturbance of April 1992); it calls for far-reaching changes in the area's urban geography. Because of the economic interdependence of Korean store owners and their Latino customers, this approach means creating a working coalition between the two. However, because of the currently complex, multiple-oppression structures, it is not easy to build coalitions between communities of color.

The case study of the Black-Korean Alliance demonstrates that when objective interests are simultaneously congruous and conflicting, dialogue alone cannot reconcile structural differences. Instead, it is necessary for such coalitions either to resolve economic issues shared by their constituents or identify points of interest that transcend divisive class interests and are not rooted in conflict. Public-space coalitions that focus on combating crime is an example of an issue that transcends class differences. Another example is a biracial or multiracial coalition that focuses on gender issues for women of color in the workplace or the media.

Two avenues of cross-racial mobilization are possible. One is to identify an issue based on the aspect that has the most potential for attracting specific constituencies from various racial and ethnic backgrounds. Organizations based on gender or labor are an example. For Korean merchants and African American residents, the issue is one of class, but there seems to be little interest in rallying around class interests, as they are conflictual despite the two groups' racial marginalization within those segments. However, one possibility for these groups is to find an issue that rises above inherent divisions and concentrates on shared interests. An example is a coalition for improving a public space. For instance, middleman minority entrepreneurs and low-income residents might be interested in eliminating mistreatment by the police department.

Summary

Conflict in Los Angeles is long standing and deeply rooted. In the case of relations between two immigrant groups, such as the Korean-Latino relations described in chapter 4, tensions emanate from relations reflecting both the economic history of a particular area and the immigrants' own political and economic experiences. Any conflict resolution approach must, therefore, take into account these considerations and make economic development and political reform part of their resolution.

Conflict resolution and community building approaches must be tailored to the community's particular needs and characteristics. It is not the case that the human relations and community development needs of south central Los Angeles will be the same as the human relations and community development needs of Pico-Union and Koreatown. The most visible difference among them is their demographics, for instance, ethnicity, socioeconomic status, and age.

Differences in ethnicity result in language differences that often add another layer of complexity. Differences in language become even more important when we consider the fact that different communities read different newspapers, each of which reports different events or even the same event but from different perspectives, which may lead to divergent rather than convergent views of daily events. In response, the Los Angeles Multicultural Collaborative proposed the creation of a "media-Rolodex," a central location where certain articles are translated for publication in other ethnic newspapers. But for ideas like this to be realized, they must be properly financed and staffed. How do we create the political and social will needed to put into operation ideas and programs that can help create common visions of community?

Different histories create different human needs. Many of the communities we have been discussing share a history of violence—Africans Americans, slavery; Central Americans, civil war; Korean Americans, occupation. These are communities of survivors, and survivors carry with them deep scars that are in the process of healing. The Salvadoran residents of Pico-Union, some of whom suffer from posttraumatic stress disorder, had to relive their own civil war during the urban unrest of 1992. Korean Americans were devastated by the realization that even here in the United States, they would once again have to carry arms to protect their property. African Americans were again enraged by the apparent loss of their right to economic self-determination. Despite their different fears and concerns, all the communities need to connect with those around them, as evidenced by many of the people we talked to who expressed a willingness to find common ground with their ethnically diverse neighbors. Indeed, many of the data presented in this text confirm for us what we intuitively knew to be true—that people will work together around common concerns that affect them on a day-to-day basis. Their willingness, however, is often difficult to transform into actual behavior when there are not enough days in the week to do the household chores and when it is sometimes all they can do just to get along with those supposedly similar to them.

The differences in intergroup dynamics across different groups also must be taken into account. The relations between blacks and Koreans emerging from the relationships between customers and merchants are different from Korean-Latino relations in Koreatown and Pico-Union emerging from cultural misunderstandings placed against the backdrop of workplace exploitation. This does not mean that cultural misunderstandings arising from language differences are not a cause of interethnic conflict, only that the specific underlying issues are different in each case. Conflict resolution and community development strategies therefore require a thorough assessment of the economic and political causes underlying racial tensions.

Tensions will continue to rise and riots will continue to erupt unless basic needs such as adequate housing, equal access to resources, and freedom from crime and violence are met. The increasing material poverty of our inner-city communities, the rapidly rising number of young men and women in prison, the continued exportation of jobs abroad, and the growing percentage of children born in poverty all make it imperative that we accept the challenge of building a multiethnic community.

Notes

1. According to this article, the suit was filed eight months after the city elections that saw the complexion of the five-member council change from mostly black to mostly Latino.

2. According to the LA 2000 projection, by the year 2010, Latinos and whites are projected to be at 40 percent each, and African Americans and Asian Americans are estimated to comprise 10 percent. In 1970, whites comprised 75 percent, Latinos 14 percent, African Americans 8 percent, and Asian Americans 3 percent of the population of Los Angeles County.

NOTES TO CHAPTER 1

1. We use the term *riots* or *civil unrest* in this book with no judgment attached. The first step in rebuilding the city and promoting multiethnic coalitions is recognizing and respecting the various communities' perspectives and voices. Many Korean American merchants and others who sustained damage during the civil disturbance feel strongly that it was a riot, whereas African American activists may emphasize the disturbance's political protest aspect and insist that it was a rebellion by a racially oppressed and underclass population. Although these different terms represent different meanings and political perspectives, we must agree to disagree and move beyond identity politics.

2. According to the Rand Corporation's computer analysis of 5,633 arrests, 51 percent of those arrested at the peak of the rioting were Latino, and 36 percent were black. The largest group was young Latino men aged eighteen to twenty-four, who accounted for 30 percent of those arrested (see Institute for Alternative Journalism 1992, p. 46).

3. The seven cities are New York (July 18–23), Rochester (N.Y.) (July 24–25), Jersey City (N.J.) (August 2–4), Paterson (N.J.) (August 11–13), Elizabeth (N.J.) (August 11–13), Chicago (August 16–17), and Philadelphia (August 28–30).

4. Plant closures since 1965 in south central Los Angeles are as follows: American Bridge in 1979, 700 employees; Bethlehem Steel in 1982, 1,600 employees; Chrysler in 1971, 2,000 employees; Discovision in 1982, 1,000 employees; Fibre-

board in 1978, 250 employees; Firestone in 1980, 1,400 employees; Ford in 1980, 2,300 employees; GM in 1982, 4,500 employees; Goodrich in 1976, 1,000 employees; Goodyear in 1980, 1,600 employees; Johns Manville in 1982, 200 employees; Lure Meat Packing in 1978, 500 employees; Max Factor in 1982, 1,000 employees; Uniroyal in 1978, 1,450 employees; and Weiser Lock in 1981, 2,100 employees.

5. In the mid-1960s, Los Angeles's auto-manufacturing industry, then the second-largest in the country, employed approximately 15,000 workers. The closing of the Van Nuys GM plant has brought that number to zero (Institute for Alternative Journalism, 1992, p. 103).

6. For a review of Guatemalan and Salvadoran community organizations, see Tomas Rivera Institute 1997.

7. In the wake of race riots in Newark and Detroit in 1967, President Lyndon B. Johnson established the National Advisory Commission on Civil Disorders headed by Governor Otto Kerner of Ohio, widely known as the Kerner Commission.

8. The gap in earnings between comparable Chicano and Anglo males in Los Angeles in 1986/87 was 20 percent and between comparable African American and Anglo males in 1988 was 30 percent (Institute for Alternative Journalism 1992, p. 120).

9. In addition, according to a Korean American InterAgency Council study, a majority of the Korean American riot victims have suffered posttraumatic stress disorder, anxiety, depression, and an increase in family problems. The Korean Family Counseling and Legal Advice Center's client caseload has climbed dramatically and remains high owing to the lingering effects of the riots. See *Korean Family Services Newsletter* 1 (Spring 1993).

10. For more information on Allen Bakke case, see Glazer 1975a.

NOTES TO CHAPTER 2

1. Of the 160 stores on 125th Street, Korean immigrants own approximately 40.

2. *The Los Angeles Sentinel* published a special editorial report on Korean–African American conflicts on the following dates: August 11, 18, and 25, and September 8, 1983.

3. Unfortunately, to promote their own causes, some people have exploited the tense relationship between Korean merchants and African American residents. It appears that *Money Talks News* has tried to appeal to African American readers by exploiting this sensitive issue. For example, it maintains that the solution to the problem is to establish an "investigative" newspaper, which *Money Talks News* claims to be. For more details, see the *Money Talks News* articles of December 12, 1984, January 1, 1985, and February 18, 1985.

4. Interview with Larry Aubry on September 22, 1988. He also made the same

statement on a KCET (the public television channel) documentary, the "Clash of Cultures," on January 17, 1987.

5. Indoor swap-meet merchants seem to be more conscious of African American customers' sensitivity and behavior. One merchant told us, "If I don't pay attention to the customer or do not greet him or her ('can I help you?'), he or she will simply walk away to another store."

6. Friedman wrote "Stereotypes in the Media" in the *San Francisco Chronicle*, May 9, 1988. It was his reaction after reading essays written by the finalists in the essay contest conducted each year by the Americanism Education League. The topic was "Dumping in International Trade: An Evil or an Opportunity?"

7. Nate Holden represents the Tenth District of the city of Los Angeles, which covers south central Los Angeles and parts of Koreatown.

8. However, it is important to note that Jews owned less than 40 percent of stores in Harlem, according to a study conducted by Levine 1968, pp. 10–12.

9. According to Yoon's (1997) survey of Korean businessmen in Los Angeles and Chicago, 62 percent relied on their personal savings in the United States as source of start-up capital. Money brought from Korea accounted for 25.6 percent in Los Angeles and 17.8 percent in Chicago.

10. According to John Higham (1978), American ethnic communities have been concerned with (1) the relationship between the United States and the groups' homelands, (2) their own status in American society, (3) the groups' internal integrity and cohesion, and (4) the essential issues of survival. The degree of importance may depend on the particular group's situation.

NOTES TO CHAPTER 3

1. All the guests were African Americans: two inactive gang members ("Bone" and "Little Monster"), a juror for the Rodney King trial, Reverend Cecil Murray of the First AME Church in Los Angeles, John Mack of the Urban League of Los Angeles, Representative Maxine Waters (Democrat representing south central Los Angeles), and Jim Gallipol, a Los Angeles County probation officer.

2. The major disputes between Korean merchants and African American customers include the "Jamaica boycott" in 1981, the "Harlem boycott" in 1984/85, and the "Brooklyn boycott" in 1988. There have been several other, smaller incidents between two groups (see Min 1996).

3. When Mr. Chang fled to the Korean-owned Church Fruit, across the street from Red Apple, African Americans boycotted both stores.

4. Interview with Mr. Man-Ho Park (August 15, 1992) an owner of Church Fruit across the street from Red Apple. The boycott spread to Church Fruit because the protesters insisted that the same person owned both stores.

5. Carson led a boycott in Bedford-Stuyvesant against a Korean store owner accused of beating a sixty-seven-year-old African American woman. He also led

several other boycotts in the city, including those in Jamaica (1981) and Harlem (1984).

6. Chung Lee served as a cochair of the Black-Korean Alliance.

7. In fact, the *Korea Times* English edition repeatedly criticized the role of mainstream media. For example, the following headlines were used by the *Korea Times Los Angeles*: "Mass Media, Agitators Fan Violence against Korean American Merchants" (April 3, 1991), "Bradley Rakes Media for Race-Mongering" (September 1, 1991), "Reactions to Du Verdict, Media Coverage" (October 21, 1991), Media under Fire for Escalating Ethnic Tensions" (November 18, 1991).

8. During the past seven years, I spoke with many African American leaders and residents of south central Los Angeles. Regardless of their education and their ideology, most of them believed that Korean immigrant merchants were receiving special government programs to purchase businesses in their own neighborhoods.

NOTES TO CHAPTER 4

1. Peter Kwong also observed that foreign capital from Taiwan and Hong Kong contributed to the rapid growth of Chinatown in New York. For more details, see Kwong 1987.

2. Interview with Roy Hong, executive director of KIWA, on March 18, 1997.

NOTES TO CHAPTER 5

1. The Multicultural Collaborative research found that one of the most effective and promising ways to reduce intergroup tension was grassroots community organizing.

2. Contrary to this statement, the Korean American community did not raise money for Mrs. Du's defense. Instead, shortly after the second shooting incident on June 4, 1991 (John's Market), the Korean American community formed the Korean American Race Relations Emergency Fund (KARE) to help the owner of John's Market (Tae Sam Park) because he faced a boycott by Danny Bakewell and his followers. The other purpose of KARE was to raise funds to support activities that improved relations between the two communities.

3. It is important to note that labor coalitions have been more successful in Los Angeles because the Korean Immigrant Workers' Advocate (KIWA) successfully fought for both Korean American and Latino workers' rights against Korean employers in Koreatown.

Bibliography

Abelmann, Nancy, and John Lie. 1995. *Blue Dreams: Korean Americans and the Los Angeles Riots*. Cambridge, Mass.: Harvard University Press.

Acuna, Rodolfo. 1981. *Occupied America: A History of Chicanos*. 2d ed. New York: Harper & Row.

Adler, P. S. 1993. "The Future of Alternative Dispute Resolution: Reflections on ADR as a Social Movement." In S. E. Merry and N. Milner, eds., *The Possibility of Popular Justice*. Ann Arbor: University of Michigan Press.

Adrian, C. R., and C. Press. 1968. "Decision Costs in Coalition Formation." *American Political Science Review* 62: 556–63.

Aguilar-San Juan, Karin. 1994. *The State of Asian America: Activism and Resistance in 1990s*. Boston: South End Press.

Ahn, Chong Sik. 1991. "An Alternative Approach to the Racial Conflict between Korean-American Small Business Owners and the Black-American Community in the New York Metropolitan Area." In Tae-Hwan Kwak and Seong Hyong Lee, eds., *The Korean-American Community: Present and Future*. Seoul: Kyung Nam University Press.

Alder, Patricia Rae. 1977. "Watts: From Suburbs to Black Ghetto" Ph.D. diss., University of Southern California.

Aldrich, Howard. 1975. "Ecological Succession in Racially Changing Neighborhoods: A Review of Literature." *Urban Affairs Quarterly* 10 (3): 327–48.

Aldrich, Howard, and A. Reiss. 1976. "Continuities in the Study of Ecological Succession: Changes in the Race Composition of Neighborhoods and Their Businessmen." *American Journal of Sociology* 81: 856–66.

Allport, Gordon. 1958. *The Nature of Prejudice*. Garden City, N.Y.: Doubleday.

Almaguer, Tomas. 1994. *Racial Fault Lines: The Historical Origins of White Supremacy in California*. Berkeley and Los Angeles: University of California Press.

Anderson, Frederick E. 1980. *The Development of Leadership and Organization Building in the Black Community of Los Angeles from 1900 through WWII*. Saratoga, Calif.: Century 21 Publishing.

Anderson, Talmadge. 1992. "Comparative Experience Factors among Black, Asian and Hispanic Americans: Coalitions or Conflicts?" *Journal of Black Studies* 23 (1): 27–38.

Aubry, Larry. 1994. "Why Are Koreans Targeted?" In Eui-Young Yu, ed., *Black-Korean Encounter: Toward Understanding and Alliance*. Los Angeles: Institute for Asian American and Pacific Asian Studies, California State University at Los Angeles.

Auster, Ellen, and Howard Aldrich. 1984. "Small Business Vulnerability: Ethnic Enclaves, and Ethnic Enterprise." In Robin Ward and Richard Jenkins, eds., *Ethnic Communities in Business*. Cambridge: Cambridge University Press.

Azar, E. E., and J. W. Burton. 1986. *International Conflict Resolution Theory and Practice*. New York: Pergamon Press.

Baird, Robert M., and Stuart E. Rosenbaum, eds. 1992. *Bigotry, Prejudice and Hatred: Definition, Causes and Solutions*. Buffalo, N.Y.: Prometheus Books.

Baldassare, Mark, ed. 1994. *The Los Angeles Riots: Lessons for the Urban Future*. Boulder, Colo.: Westview Press.

Baldwin, James. 1967. "Negroes Are Anti-Semitic Because They're Anti-White." *New York Times Magazine*, April 9, p. 27.

Banks, J. A. 1986. "Multicultural Education and Its Critics: Britain and the United States." In S. Modgil, G. K. Verma, and K. Mallick, eds., *Multicultural Education: The Interminable Debate*. Philadelphia: Falmer Press.

Banton, Michael. 1983. *Racial and Ethnic Competition*. Cambridge: Cambridge University Press.

Barrera, Mario. 1979. *Race and Class in the Southwest*. Notre Dame, Ind.: Notre Dame University Press.

Barringer, Herbert R., and Sung-Nam Cho. 1989. *Koreans in the United States: A Fact Book*. Honolulu: Center for Korean Studies, University of Hawaii.

Bass, Karen. 1992. "Liquor Stores: Give a Helping Hand to Owners." *Los Angeles Times*, November 23.

Becker, Gary S. 1979. *The Economics of Discrimination*. Chicago: University of Chicago Press.

Bender, Eugene J. 1969. "Reflections on Negro-Jewish Relationships: The Historical Dimension." *Phylon* 30 (Spring): 56–65.

Benedixen & Associate. 1993. *Public Opinion Survey of Residents of South Central Los Angeles and Pico-Union*. Washington, D.C., and Los Angeles: Benedixen & Associate.

Berreman, Gerald. 1960. "Caste in India and the United States." *American Journal of Sociology* 66 (September): 120–27.

Blalock, Hubert M., Jr. 1967. *Toward a Theory of Minority Group Relations*. New York: Wiley.

Blauner, Robert. 1969. "Whitewash over Watts: The Failure of McCone Commission Report." In Robert M. Fogelson, ed., *Mass Violence in America: The Los Angeles Riots*. New York: *New York Times*.

———. 1972. *Racial Oppression in America*. New York: Harper & Row.

———. 1989. *Black Lives and White Lives*. Berkeley and Los Angeles: University of California Press.

Bluestone, Barry, and Bennette Harrison, eds. 1982. *The Deindustrialization of America*. New York: Basic Books.

Bonacich, Edna. 1973. "A Theory of Middleman Minorities." *American Sociological Review* 38 (October): 583–94.

———. 1988. "The Social Costs of Immigrant Entrepreneurship." *Amerasia Journal* 14 (1): 119–28.

———.1989. "The Role of the Petite Bourgeoisie within Capitalism: A Response to Pyong Gap Min." *Amerasia Journal* 15 (2): 195–203.

Bonacich, Edna, and Taewhan Jung 1982. "A Portrait of Korean Small Business in Los Angeles: 1977." In Eui Young Yu, E. Phillips, and E. S. Yang, eds., *Koreans in Los Angeles*. Los Angeles: Center for Korean-American and Korean Studies, California State University at Los Angeles.

Bonacich, Edna, and John Modell. 1980. *The Economic Basis of Ethnic Solidarity: Small Business in the Japanese American Community*. Berkeley and Los Angeles: University of California Press.

Borchert, James. 1980. *Alley Life in Washington*. Champaign-Urbana: University of Illinois Press.

Bowles, Samuel, and Herbert Gintis. 1975. "The Problem with Human Capital Theory: A Marxist Interpretation." *American Economic Review* 65 (May): 74–82.

Boyarsky, Bill. "Korean-Americans Ask Why Recovery Is Black and White." *Los Angeles Times*, March 14, 1993.

Boyd, Robert. 1990. "Black and Asian Self-Employment in Large Metropolitan Areas: A Comparative Analysis." *Social Problems* 37: 258–74.

Brass, Paul R., ed. 1996. *Riots and Pogroms*. London: Macmillan.

Brecher, Jeremy, and Tim Costello eds. 1990. *Building Bridges: The Emerging Grassroots Coalition of Labor and Community*. New York: Monthly Review Press.

Brotz, Howard. 1964. *The Black Jews of Harlem: Negro Nationalism and the Dilemmas of Negro Leadership*. New York: Free Press.

Browning, Rufus P., Dale Rogers Marshall, and David H. Tabb, eds. 1984. *Protest Is Not Enough: The Struggle of Blacks and Hispanics for Equality in City Politics*. Berkeley and Los Angeles: University of California Press.

———. 1990. *Racial Politics in American Cities*. New York: Longman.

Budge, Lan, and Hans Keman. 1990. *Parties and Democracy: Coalition Formation and Government Function in Twenty States*. Oxford: Oxford University Press.

Bullard, Robert D., ed. 1993. *Confronting Environmental Racism: Voices from the Grassroost*. Boston: South End Press.

Bunch, L. 1992. "A Past Not Necessarily Prologue: The Afro-American in Los

Angeles." In N. M. Klein and M. J. Schiels, eds., *20th Century Los Angeles: Power, Promotion, and Social Conflict*. Claremont, Calif.: Regina Books.

Bush, R. B., and J. P. Folger. 1994. *The Promise of Mediation*. San Francisco: Jossey-Bass.

Calderon, Jose. 1990. "Latinos and Ethnic Conflict in Suburbia: The Case of Monterey Park." *Latino Studies Journal* 2: 23–32.

Caplow, T. 1968. *Two Against One: Coalitions in Triads*. Englewood Cliffs, N.J.: Prentice-Hall.

Camarillo, Albert. 1979. *Chicanos in a Changing Society: From Mexican Pueblos to American Barrios in Santa Barbara and Southern California, 1848–1930*. Cambridge, Mass.: Harvard University Press.

Carmichael, Stokely, and Charles Hamilton. 1967. *Black Power: The Politics of Liberation in America*. New York: Vintage Books.

Case, F. E. 1972. *Black Capitalism: Problems in Development, a Case Study of Los Angeles*. New York: Praeger.

Chan, Sucheng. 1986. *Bitter-Sweet Soil: The Chinese in California Agriculture, 1860–1910*. Berkeley and Los Angeles: University of California Press.

———. 1991. *Asian Americans: An Interpretive History*. Boston: Twayne.

Chang, Edward T. 1990. "New Urban Crisis: Korean-Black Conflict in Los Angeles." Ph.D. diss., University of California at Berkeley.

———. 1992. "Building Minority Coalitions: A Case Study of Korean and African Americans." *Korea Journal of Population and Development* 21 (July): 37–56.

———. 1993. "Jewish and Korean Merchants in African American Neighborhoods: A Comparative Perspective." *Amerasia Journal* 19 (2): 5–22.

———. 1994a. "America's First Multiethnic Riots." In Karin Aguilar-San Juan, ed., *State of Asian America: Activism and Resistance in the 1990s*. Boston: South End Press.

———. 1994b. "An Emerging Minority Seeks a Role in a Changing America." *Los Angeles Times*, May 31.

———. 1994c. "Myths and Realities of Korean-Black American Relations." In Eui-Young Yu, ed., *Black-Korean Encounter: Toward Understanding and Alliance*. Los Angeles: Institute for Asian American and Pacific Asian Studies, California State University at Los Angeles.

———. 1995. "The Impact of the Civil Unrest on Community-Based Organizational Coalitions." In Eui-Young Yu and Edward T. Chang, eds., *Multiethnic Coalition Building in L.A.* Claremont, Calif.: Regina Books.

———. 1996a. "African American Boycotts of Korean-Owned Stores in New York and Los Angeles." In Paul R. Brass, ed., *Riots and Pogroms*. London: Macmillan.

———. 1996b. "Toward Understanding Korean and African American Relations." *OAH Magazine of History*, Summer, pp. 67–71.

Chang, Edward T., and Russell C. Leong, eds. 1994. *Los Angeles—Struggles toward Multiethnic Community*. Seattle: University of Washington Press.

Chang, Edward T., and Angela Eunjin Oh. 1994. "The Messengers Are Sending Wrong Signals to L.A." *Los Angeles Times*, April 7.

———. 1995. "Korean American Dilemma: Violence, Vengeance, Vision." In Dean A. Harris, ed., *Multiculturalism from the Margins*. Westport, Conn.: Bergin & Garvey.

Chang, Edward T., and Eui-Young. 1994. "Chronology of Black-Korean Encounter." In Eui-Young Yu, ed., *Black-Korean Encounter: Toward Understanding and Alliance*. Los Angeles: Institute for Asian American and Pacific Asian Studies, California State University at Los Angeles.

Chang, Jeff. 1994. "Race, Class, Conflict, and Empowerment: On the Ice Cube's Black Korea." *Amerasia Journal* 19 (2): 87–102.

Chen, Elsa Y. 1991. "Black-Led Boycotts of Korean-Owned Grocery Stores." Senior thesis, Princeton University.

Cheng, Lucie, and Yen Le Espiritu. 1989. "Korean Business in Black and Hispanic Neighborhoods: A Study of Intergroup Relations." *Sociological Perspectives* 32: 521–34.

Cherry, Robert. 1989. "Middleman Minority Theories: Their Implications for Black-Jewish Relations." *Journal of Ethnic Studies* 17 (4): 117–38.

Chertkoff, J. M. 1975. "Sociopsychological Views on Sequential Effects in Coalition Formation." *American Behavioral Scientist* 18 (4): 451–71.

Chinchilla, N., and N. Hamilton. 1989. *Central American Enterprise in Los Angeles*. New Direction for Latino Public Policy Research, Working Paper no. 6, Center for Mexican American Studies, University of Texas at Austin.

———. 1997. *Ambiguous Identities: Central Americans in Southern California*. Working Paper no. 14, Chicano/Latino Research Center, University of California at Santa Cruz.

Cho, Sumi K. 1993. "Korean American vs. African Americans: Conflict and Construction." In Robert Gooding-Williams, ed., *Reading Rodney King/Reading Urban Uprising*. New York: Routledge.

Choi, Alice H. 1993. "A Closer Look at the Conflict between the African-Americans and the Korean American Communities in South Central Los Angeles." *Asian American Pacific Islands Law Journal* 1 (February): 69–78.

Choy, Bong-Youn. 1979. *Koreans in America*. Chicago: Nelson-Hall.

Chung, Angie. 1995. "Formation of Third World Consciousness among Coalitions of Color: Multi-Oppression Politics from the 1960s to the Present." Senior thesis, Yale University.

Chung, John. 1992. "Report on Coverage of the Korean American Community by the Los Angeles Times." Report presented to the Korean American Bar Association Media Relations Committee, Los Angeles, June.

Chung, Joseph. 1979. "Small Ethnic Business as a Form of Disguised Unemployment and Cheap Labor." In U.S. Commission on Civil Rights, *Civil Rights Issues of Asian & Pacific Americans: Myth and Realities.* Washington, D.C.: U.S. Commission on Civil Rights, March.

Chung, Philip W. 1993. "Hate Crimes against KAs (Korean Americans) Highest among Asians." *Korea Times* English Edition. March 31.

Clark, Kenneth. 1946. "Candor about Negro-Jewish Relations." *Commentary*, February, pp. 8–14.

———. 1967. *Dark Ghetto: Dilemmas of Social Power.* New York: Harper & Row.

Clark, William A. V. 1993. "Neighborhood Transitions in Multiethnic/Racial Context." *Journal of Urban Affairs* 15 (2):161–72.

Cleaver, James H. 1983a. "Asian Attitudes toward Blacks Cause Raised Eyebrows." *Los Angeles Sentinel*, August 18.

———. 1983b. "Asian Business in Black Community Causes Stir." *Los Angeles Sentinel*, August 11.

———. 1983c. "Black Agenda Hosts Korean Dialogue." *Los Angeles Sentinel*, September 15.

———. 1983d. "Citizens Air Gripes about Asian." *Los Angeles Sentinel*, September 1.

———. 1983e. "Residents Complain about Alleged Asian Problem." *Los Angeles Sentinel*, August 2.

Clinica Monseñor Oscar A. Romero (n.d.). *Pico-Union/Westlake Profile.* Los Angeles.

Cohen, Nathan. 1970. *The Los Angeles Riots: A Sociological Study.* New York: Praeger.

Coleman, Wanda. 1993. "Remembering Latasha: Blacks, Immigrants and America." *The Nation*, February 15, pp. 187–91.

Coles, Flournay A., Jr. 1975. *Black Economic Development.* Chicago: Nelson Hall.

Collins, Keith. 1980. *Black Los Angeles: The Maturing of the Ghetto: 1940–1950.* Saratoga, Calif.: Century 21 Publishing.

Collins, Patricia Hill. 1993. "Black Feminist Thought in the Matrix of Domination." In C. Lemert, ed., *Social Theory.* Boulder, Colo.: Westview Press.

Cone, James. 1969. *Black Religion and Black Power.* New York: Seabury Press.

Cornacchia, Eugene J., and Dale C. Nelson. 1992. "Historical Differences in the Political Experiences of American Blacks and White Ethnics: Revisiting and Unresolved Controversy." *Ethnic and Racial Studies* 15 (1): 102–22.

Cox, Oliver. 1948. *Caste, Class and Race: A Study in Social Dynamics.* New York: Doubleday.

Crenshaw, Kimberlé, 1989. "Demarginalizing the Intersection of Race and Sex: A Black Feminist Critique of Antidiscrimination Doctrine, Feminist Theory and Antiracist Politics." *University of Chicago Legal Forum*, pp. 139–67.

Crump, Spencer. 1966. *Black Riots in Los Angeles: The Story of the Watts Tragedy.* Los Angeles: Trans-Anglo Books.

Cruse, Harold. 1967. *The Crisis of Negro Intellectual.* New York: Morrow.

————. 1987. *Plural but Equal: A Critical Study of Blacks and Minorities and America's Plural Society*. New York: Morrow.

Davis, Mike. 1992. *City of Quartz: Excavating the Future in Los Angeles*. New York: Vintage Books.

Dawes, R. M. 1980. "Social Dilemmas." *Annual Review of Psychology* 31: 169–93.

DeConde, Alexander. 1992. *Ethnicity, Race, and American Foreign Policy: A History*. Boston: Northeastern University Press.

de Graaf, Lawrence B. 1962. "Negro Migration to Los Angeles, 1930–1950." Ph.D. diss., University of California at Los Angeles.

————. 1970. "The City of Black Angels: Emergence of the Los Angeles Ghetto, 1890–1930." *Pacific Historical Review* 39: 323–52.

Delgado, Gary. 1993. "Building Multiracial Alliances: The Case of People United for a Better Oakland." In R. Fisher and J. Kling, eds., *Mobilizing the Community*. Newbury Park, Calif.: Sage.

Delgado, H. L. 1993. *New Immigrants, Old Unions*. Philadelphia: Temple University Press.

Department of Employment Development, State of California. 1993. *Analysis of the 1992 Los Angeles Civil Unrest*. Los Angeles: Department of Employment Development, February.

Diaz-Veizades, Jeannette. 1993. "Social Psychological Dynamics of African American and Korean American Relations in Los Angeles." Ph.D. diss., University of California at Riverside.

Diaz-Veizades, Jeannette, and Edward T. Chang. 1996. "Building Cross-Cultural Coalitions: A Case Study of the Black-Korean Alliance and the Latino-Black Roundtable." *Ethnic and Racial Studies* 19 (July): 680–700.

Dixon, Marlene, and Susanne Jonas, eds. 1982. *The New Normads*. San Francisco: Synthesis Publications.

Doherty, Jake. 1992. "Black-Korean Alliance Says Talk Not Enough, Disbands." *Los Angeles Times*, December 24.

Donald, James, and Ali Rattansi, eds. 1992. *"Race," Culture and Difference*. London: Sage.

Duster, Troy. 1990. *Diversity Project* (final report). Center for the Study of Social Change, University of California at Berkeley.

Edwards, Richard C. 1979. *Contested Terrain*. New York: Basic Books.

Edwards, Richard, Michael Reich, and David M. Gordon. "A Theory of Labor Market Segmentation." *American Economic Review* 63 (May): 359–65.

Elazar, Daniel, and Murray Friedman. 1976. *Moving Up: Ethnic Succession in America*. New York: Institute on Pluralism and Group Identity.

Espiritu, Yen Le. 1992. *Asian American Panethnicity: Bridging Institutions and Identities*. Philadelphia: Temple University Press.

"Extraordinary Collection of Letters on Racism Tells of Tears, Pride, Puzzlement." 1993. *Asian Week*, May 28, pp. 14–15.

Fairs, Gerald, and Ashley Dunn. 1991. "Anti-Karlin Protesters Enter Courthouse." *Los Angeles Times*, December 13.

Farber, M. A. 1990. "Black-Korean Who-Pushed-Whom Festers, Blemishing the Gorgeous Mosaic." *New York Times*, May 7.

Ferretti, Fred. 1969. "New York's Black Anti-Semitism Scare." *Columbia Journalism Review*, Fall.

Fong, Timothy P. 1989. "The Unique Convergence: Monterey Park." *California Sociologist* 12 (Summer): 171–93.

———. 1994. *The First Suburban Chinatown: The Remaking of Monterey Park, California.* Philadelphia: Temple University Press.

Ford, Andrea, and John H. Lee. 1991a. "Racial Tensions Blamed in Girl's Death." *Los Angeles Times*, March 20.

———. 1991b. "Slain Girl Was Not Stealing Juice, Police Say." *Los Angeles Times*, March 19.

Foster, M. 1978. "Black Organizing: The Need for a Conceptual Model of the Ghetto." *Catalyst* 1 (1): 76.

Frankenberg, Ruth. *White Women, Race Matters.* Minneapolis: University of Minnesota Press.

Franklin, John H. 1980. *From Slavery to Freedom.* New York: Knopf.

Fredrickson, George M. 1981. *White Supremacy: A Comparative Study in American and South African History.* Oxford: Oxford University Press.

Freeman, Mike. 1992. "Riots Boost May Ratings in L.A." *Broadcasting.* June, pp. 20–22.

Freer, Regina. 1994. "Black-Korean Conflict." In Mark Baldassare, ed., *The Los Angeles Riots.* Boulder, Colo.: Westview Press.

Freire, Paulo. 1974. *Pedagogy of the Oppressed.* New York: Continuum.

Fuchs, L. 1991. *The American Kaleidoscope: Race, Ethnicity and the Civic Culture.* Hanover, N.H.: Wesleyan University Press.

Furnivall, J. S. 1948. *Colonial Policy and Practice: A Comparative Study of Burma and Netherland India.* Cambridge: Cambridge University Press.

Gamson, W. A. 1961. "A Theory of Coalition Formation." *American Sociological Review* 26: 373–82.

Gans, Herbert J. 1973. "Negro-Jewish Conflict in New York City." In D. E. Gelfand and R. D. Lee, eds., *Ethnic Conflicts and Power: A Cross-National Perspective.* New York: Wiley.

———. 1993. "From 'Underclass' to 'Undercaste': Some Observations about the Future of the Postindustrial Economy and Its Major Victims." *International Journal of Urban and Regional Research* 17 (September): 327–35.

Gardner, Robert. 1992. *Asian Immigration: The View from the United States.* Honolulu: East-West Center, University of Hawaii.

Gee, Emma, ed. 1976. *Counterpoint: Perspectives on Asian America.* Los Angeles: Asian American Studies Center, University of California.

Gentry, M. E. 1987. "Coalition Formation and Processes." *Social Work with Groups* 10 (3): 39–54.

Giliam, Frank D. 1996. "Exploring Minority Empowerment: Symbolic Politics, Governing Coalitions, and Traces of Political Style in Los Angeles." *American Journal of Political Science* 40 (February): 56–81.

Gilroy, Paul. 1987. *There Ain't No Black in the Union Jack.* Chicago: University of Chicago Press.

Gitlin, Todd. 1993a. "From Universality to Difference: Notes on the Fragmentation of the Idea of the Left." *Contention* 2 (2): 15–40.

———. 1993b. "The Rise of Identity Politics." *Dissent,* Spring, pp. 172–77.

Givens, Helen. "The Korean Community in Los Angeles." Master's thesis, University of Southern California.

Glazer, Nathan. 1993. "School Wars: A Brief History of Multiculturalism in America." *Brookings Review* 11 (4): 16H–20.

———. 1969. "Blacks, Jews, and the Intellectuals." *Commentary.* January, pp. 33–39.

———. 1975a. *Affirmative Discrimination: Ethnic Inequality and Public Policy.* New York: Basic Books.

———. 1975b. *Ethnicity: Theory and Experience.* Cambridge, Mass.: Harvard University Press.

———. 1993. "Is Assimilation Dead?" *Annals of the American Academy of Political and Social Science* 530 (November): 122–27.

Glazer, Nathan, and Daniel Moynihan 1963. *Beyond the Melting Pot: Negroes, Puerto Ricans, Jews, Italians, and Irish of New York City.* Cambridge, Mass.: MIT Press.

Goldberg, David Theo, ed. 1990. *Anatomy of Racism.* Minneapolis: University of Minnesota Press.

Gonzales, Jual L., Jr. 1993. "Race Relations in the United States." *Humboldt Journal of Social Relations* 19 (2): 39–78.

Gooding-Williams, Robert F. 1993. *Reading Rodney King/Reading Urban Uprising.* New York: Routledge.

Gordon, Milton. 1963. *Assimilation in American Life.* New York: Oxford University Press.

Gossett, Thomas. 1965. *Race: The History of an Idea in America.* New York: Schocken Books.

Gotanda, Neil. "Reading *People v. Soon Ja Du* (The Latasha Harlins Case): Racial Stratification in a 'Color Blind' Sentencing Colloquy." Unpublished manuscript. Western State University College of Law (Fullerton, Calif.)

Grant, Jaime M. 1996. "Building Community-Based Coalitions from Academe: The Union Institute and the Kitchen Table: Women of Color Press Transition Coalition." *Signs,* Summer, pp. 1024–33.

Gray, J. S., and A. J. Thompson. 1953. "Ethnic Prejudices of White and Negro College Students." *Journal of Abnormal and Social Psychology* 48: 311–13.

Greenberg, Stanley B. 1980. *Race & State in Capitalist Development: Comparative Perspective*. New Haven, Conn.: Yale University Press.

Hacker, Andrew. 1992. *Two Nations: Black, and White, Separate, Hostile, Unequal*. New York: Scribner.

Hall, Stuart. 1990. "Cultural Identity and Diaspora." In Jonathan Rutherford, ed., *Identity, Community, Culture, Difference*. London: Lawrence.

Hamilton, Charles. 1975. "The Patron-Recipient Relationship and Minority Politics in New York City." *Political Science Quarterly* 95 (2): 211–27.

Harap, Louis. 1942. "Anti-Negroism among Jews." *Negro Quarterly* 1 (Summer): 105–11.

Harrington, Michael. 1984. *New American Poverty*. New York: Holt, Rinehart and Winston.

Harris, Dean A., ed. 1995. *Multiculturalism from the Margins: Non-Dominant Voices on Difference and Diversity*. Westport, Conn.: Bergin & Garvey.

Hayes-Bautista, 1993. *Chartbook of Ethnic and Racial Groups Health and Medical Care Indicator for Los Angeles County*. Los Angeles: Center of Excellence, UCLA School of Medicine.

Hayes-Bautista, David E., Werner O. Schink, and Maria Hayes-Bautista. 1993. "Latinos and the 1992 Los Angeles Riots: A Behavioral Sciences Perspective." *Hispanic Journal of Behavioral Sciences* 15 (4): 427–48.

Henry, Charles P. 1980. "Black-Chicano Coalitions: Possibilities and Problems." *Western Journal of Black Studies* 4: 202–32.

———. 1990. *Culture and African American Politics*. Bloomington: Indiana University Press.

———. 1992. "Understanding the Underclass: The Role of Culture and Economic Progress." In James Jenning, ed., *Race, Politics, and Economic Development: Community Perspectives*. London: Verso.

Hentoff, Nat. 1969. "Blacks and Jews: An Interview with Julius Lester." *Evergreen Review*, April, p. 21.

———, ed. 1970. *Black Anti-Semitism and Jewish Racism*. New York: Schocken Books.

Herbert, Solomon J. 1992. "Why African-Americans Vented Anger at the Korean Community during the LA Riots." *Crisis*, August–September, p. 38.

Hicks, Joe 1994. "Rebuilding in the Wake of Rebellion: The Need for Economic Conversion." in Eui-Young Yu, ed., *Black-Korean Encounter: Toward Understanding and Alliance*. Los Angeles: Institute for Asian American and Pacific Asian Studies, California State University at Los Angeles.

Higham, John. 1978. *Ethnic Leadership in America*. Baltimore: Johns Hopkins University Press.

Hill, R. 1995. "Overview of Dispute Resolution." rhill@batnet.com.

Hing, Bill Ong. 1993. *Making and Remaking Asian America through Immigration Policy, 1850–1990*. Stanford, Calif.: Stanford University Press.

Hirsch, Arnold. 1983. *Making the Second Ghetto*. Cambridge: Cambridge University Press.

Hirschberg, Ted, ed. 1981. *Philadelphia*. New York: Oxford University Press.

Hofstadter, Richard. 1955. *Social Darwinism in American Thought, 1860–1915*. Rev. ed. Boston: Beacon Press.

Hook, Bell. 1990. *Yearning: Race, Gender, and Cultural Politics*. Boston: South End Press.

Horne, Gerald. 1995. *Fire This Time: The Watts Uprising and the 1960s*. Charlottesville: University Press of Virginia.

————. 1997. "America's New Racial Divide Is East-West, Not North-South." *Los Angeles Times*, August 24.

Horton, John. 1995. *The Politics of Diversity: Immigration, Resistance, and Change in Monterey Park, California*. Philadelphia: Temple University Press.

Houston, Velina Hasu. 1990. "The Fallout over 'Miss Saigon.'" *Los Angeles Times*, August 13.

Hurh, Won Moo, and Kwang Chung Kim. 1984. *Korean Immigrants in America: A Structural Analysis of Ethnic Confinement and Adhesive Adaptation*. Madison, N.J.: Fairleigh Dickinson University Press.

Hurtado, Aida. 1992. "Redefining California: Latino Social Engagement in a Multicultural Society." Los Angeles: UCLA Chicano Studies Research Center.

Hutchinson, E. O. 1991. "Fighting the Wrong Enemy." *The Nation*, November, pp. 554–55.

Hwangbo, Kay. 1992. "Protesters Hurt by Latest Attacks." *Korea Times*, July 13.

Ichioka, Yuji. 1988. *The Issei: The World of the First Generation Japanese Immigrants, 1885–1924*. New York: Free Press.

Im, Yongjin. 1992. "Media Bias Aggravated Riot Damage." *KoreAm Journal*, September, p. 28.

Institute for Alternative Journalism. 1992. *Inside the L.A. Riots: What Really Happened and Why It Will Happen Again*. New York: Institute for Alternative Journalism.

Iritani, Evelyn. 1995. "L.A. Surpasses New York City as Top Trade Hub in 1994." *Los Angeles Times*, March 17.

Jackson, Byran O. 1991. "Racial and Ethnic Voting Cleavages in Los Angeles Politics." In Byran O. Jackson and Michael B. Preston, eds., *Racial and Ethnic Politics in California*. Berkeley, Calif.: Institute of Governmental Studies.

Jackson, Byran O., and Michael B. Preston, eds. 1991. *Racial and Ethnic Politics in California*. Berkeley, Calif.: Institute of Governmental Studies.

Jacobs, Paul. 1966. "Negro-Jewish Relations in America." *Midstream*. December.

Jenning, James. 1992. "New Urban Racial and Ethnic Conflicts in the United States Politics." *Sage Race Relations Abstracts* 17 (August): 3–36.

Jensen, Arthur. 1969. "How Much Can We Boost I.Q. and Scholastic Achievement?" *Harvard Educational Review* 39: 1–123.

Jo, Moon H. 1992. "Korean Merchants in the Black Community: Prejudice among the Victims of Prejudice." *Ethnic and Racial Studies* 15 (July): 395–411.

Johnson, James, Jr., et al. 1992. "The Los Angeles Rebellion: A Retrospective View." *Economic Development Quarterly* 6 (November): 356–72.

Johnson, James, Jr., and Melvin Oliver. 1984. "Interethnic Minority Conflict in Urban America: The Effects of Economic and Social Dislocations." *Urban Geography* 10 (September–October): 449–63.

Jonas, S. 1996. *Transnational Realities and Anti-Immigrant State Policies: Issues Raised by the Experiences of Central American Immigrants and Refugees in a Transnational Region.* Working Paper no. 7. Santa Cruz: Chicano Latino Research Center, University of California.

Jones, Solomon. 1969. "The Government Riots of Los Angeles." Master's thesis, University of Southern California.

Jordon, Winthrop. 1968. *White over black: American Attitudes toward the Negro, 1550–1812.* Chapel Hill: University of North Carolina Press.

Kang, K. Connie. 1992. "Koreans Confront a Need for Change." *Los Angeles Times,* November 16.

———. 1993a. "Fear of Crime Robs Many of Dreams in Koreatown." *Los Angeles Times,* June 21.

———. 1993b. "40 percent of Koreans in Poll Ponder Leaving." *Los Angeles Times,* March 19.

———. 1993c. "Korean Riot Victims Still Devastated." *Los Angeles Times,* July 23.

———. 1998. "Ex-Workers' Suit Seeks Back Wages." *Los Angeles Times,* August 5.

Katz, Jesse. 1992. "The Times Poll: Asking Ourselves." *Los Angeles Times,* November 16.

Katz, Shlomo, ed. 1967. *Negro and Jew: An Encounter in America.* New York: Macmillan.

Katznelson, Ira. 1981. *City Trenches.* New York: Pantheon Books.

Kerner Commission. 1988. *The Kerner Report: The 1988 Report of the National Advisory Commission on Civil Disorders.* New York: Pantheon Books.

Kim, Bong Hwan. 1995. "Issues of Community-Based Joint Economic Ventures." In Eui-Young Yu and Edward T. Chang, eds., *Multiethnic Coalition Building in Los Angeles.* Los Angeles: Institute for Asian American and Pacific American Studies, California State University at Los Angeles.

Kim, Elain H. 1993. "Home Is Where the Han Is: A Korean American Perspective on the Los Angeles Upheaval." *Social Justice* 20 (1 and 2): 1–21.

———. 1994. "Between Black and White: An Interview with Bong Hwan Kim." In Karin Aguilar-San Juan, ed., *The State of Asian America: Activism and Resistance in the 1990s.* Boston: South End Press.

Kim, Hyung Chan, ed. 1977. *The Korean Diaspora: Historical and Sociological Studies of Korean Immigration and Assimilation in North America.* Santa Barbara, Calif.: ABC Clio.

Kim, Hyung Chan, and Eun Ho Lee, eds. 1990. *Koreans in America; Dreams and Realities.* Seoul, Korea: Institute for Korean Studies.

Kim, Illsoo. 1981. *New Urban Immigrants: The Korean Community in New York.* Princeton, N.J.: Princeton University Press.

Kim, Kwang Chung, and Won Moo Hurh. 1983. "Korean Americans and the 'Success' Image: A Critique." *Amerasia Journal* 10 (2): 3–21.

———. 1985. "Ethnic Resources Utilization of Korean Small Businessmen in the United States." *International Migration Review* 19: 82–111.

Kim, Elaine H., and Eui-Young Yu, eds. 1996. *East to America: Korean American Life Stories.* New York: New Press.

Kochiyama, Yuri. 1992. "Malcolm X." *Korea Times* English Edition, November 25.

Komorita, S. S. 1974. "A Weighed Probability Model of Coalition Formation." *Psychological Review* 81: 242–56.

Komorita, S. S., and J. M. Chertkoff. 1973. "A Bargaining Theory of Coalition Formation." *Psychological Review* 80: 149–62.

Koo, Hagen, and Eui-Young Yu. 1981. "Korean Immigration to the United States: Its Demographic Pattern and Social Implications for Both Societies." Papers of the East-West Population Institute, no. 74. Honolulu: East-West Center, University of Hawaii.

Korean Immigrant Workers Advocates. 1997. *Koreatown Restaurant Workers Justice Campaign Update*, October 20.

Kotkin, Joel. 1997. "Can Pico-Union Become Like N.Y.'s Lower East Side?" *Los Angeles Times*, September 28.

Kraybill, R. 1995. "Development, Conflict Resolution and the RDP." *Track Two*, September.

Kwak, Tae-Hwan, and Seong Hyong Lee eds. 1990. *The Korean-American Community: Present and Future.* Seoul, Korea: Kyungnam University Press.

Kwon, Ho-Yeon, and Shin Kim, eds. 1993. *The Emerging Generation of Korean Americans.* Seoul, Korea: Kyung Hee University Press.

Kwong, Peter. 1979. *Chinatown, New York: Labor and Politics, 1930–1950.* New York: Monthly Review Press.

———. 1987. *The New Chinatown.* New York: Noonday Press.

———. 1992. "The First Multicultural Riots." *Village Voice*, June 9.

Lacey, Marc. 1992. "Last Call for Liquor Outlets?" *Los Angeles Times*, December 14.

Lee, Dong Ok. 1995. "Koreatown and Korean Small Firms in Los Angeles: Locating in the Ethnic Neighborhoods." *Professional Geographer* 47 (2): 184–95.

Lee, Gary, and Roberto Suro. 1993. "Latino-Black Rivalry Grows." *Washington Post*, October 13, 1993.

Lee, Heon Chol. 1993. "Korean-Black Conflict in New York City: A Sociological Analysis." Ph.D. diss., Columbia University.

Lee, June. 1993. "Perspectives from the Playground: Korean-American Children Sound off on the Uprising." *Pacific Ties* (UCLA's Asian and Pacific Islander newsmagazine), April, p. 15.

Lee, Ki-Baek. 1984. *A New History of Korea.* Cambridge, Mass.: Harvard University Press.

Lee, Mary Paik. 1990. *Quiet Odyssey: A Pioneer Korean Woman in America.* Seattle: University of Washington Press.

Leonard, Jack. 1998. "$800-Million Civil Rights Suit Filed against City of Lynwood," *Los Angeles Times,* August 13.

Levine, Naomi. 1968. "Who Owns the Stores in Harlem." *Congress Bi-Weekly,* September 16.

Lewis, Oscar. 1966. "The Culture of Poverty." *Scientific American* 215: 19–25.

Liberson, Stanley. 1983. *A Piece of the Pie: American Attitudes toward the Negro, 1550–1812.* Chapel Hill: University of North Carolina Press.

Light, Ivan. 1972. *Ethnic Enterprise in America: Business and Welfare among Chinese, Japanese and Blacks.* Berkeley and Los Angeles: University of California Press.

Light, Ivan, and Edna Bonacich. 1988. *Immigrant Entrepreneurs: Koreans in Los Angeles.* Berkeley and Los Angeles: University of California Press.

Light, Ivan, and Carolyn Rosenstein. 1995. *Race, Ethnicity and Entrepreneurship in Urban America.* New York: Aldine De Gruyter.

Loewen, James. 1971. *The Mississippi Chinese: Between Black and White.* Cambridge, Mass.: Harvard University Press.

Lopez, D., E. Poppin, and E. Telles. 1995. "To Earn a Living: The Occupational World of Central American Immigrants in Los Angeles." Paper presented at Conference of Central Americans in California., University of Southern California.

Los Angeles 2000 Committee. 1988. *Los Angeles 2000: A City for the Future.* Final Report of the Los Angeles 2000 Committee.

Lowe, Lisa. "Heterogeneity, Hybridity, Multiplicity: Making Asian American Differences." *Diaspora* 1: 24–44.

Lubasch, Arnold H. 1991. "Korean Grocer Acquitted by Jury in Case That Ignited Long Boycott." *New York Times,* January 31.

Lubiano, Wahneema. 1992. "Multiculturalism: Negotiating Politics and Knowledge." *Concerns* 22 (3): 11–21.

Madhubuti, Kaki R., ed. 1993. *Why L.A. Happened: Implications of the '92 Los Angeles Rebellion.* Chicago: Third World Press.

Malcolm X. 1966. *The Autobiography of Malcolm X.* New York: Grove Press.

Marable, Manning. 1980. *From the Grass Roots.* Boston: South End Press.

―――. 1983. *How Capitalism Underdeveloped Black America.* Boston: South End Press.

Markus, Hazel, and S. Kitayama. 1991. "Culture and the Self: Implications for Cognition, Emotion, and Motivation." *Psychological Review* 98 (2): 224–53.

Marx, Gary. 1967. *Protest and Prejudice: A Study of Belief in the Black Community.* New York: Harper & Row.

May, Meredith. 1993. "Working through the Pain." *Bay Guardian,* March 31, pp. 21–23.

McCone Commission Report 1965. "Violence in the City—An End or a Beginning?" A Report by the Governor's Commission on the Los Angeles Riots, December 2.

Meier, A. and Rudwick, Elliot. 1970. *From Plantation to Ghetto.* New York: Hill & Wang.

Messaris, Paul, and Jisuk Woo. 1991. "Image vs. Reality in Korean-Americans' Responses to Mass-Mediated Depictions of the United States." *Critical Studies in Mass Communication* 8: 74–90.

Miles, J. 1992. "Black vs. Browns. *Atlantic Monthly.* October.

Min, Pyong Gap. 1988. *Minority Business Enterprise: Korean Small Business in Atlanta.* Staten Island, N.Y.: Center for Migration Studies.

―――. 1989. "The Social Costs of Immigrant Entrepreneurship: A Response to Edna Bonacich." *Amerasia Journal* 15 (2): 187–94.

―――. 1990. "Problems of Korean Immigrant Entrepreneurs." *International Migration Review* 24 (Fall): 436–55.

―――. 1994. "The Middleman Minority Characteristic of Korean Immigrants in the United States." *Korea Journal of Population and Development* 23: 179–202.

―――― 1996. *Caught in the Middle: Korean Communities in New York and Los Angeles.* Berkeley and Los Angeles: University of California Press.

Mitchell, M. 1991. "Police Keep Watch at Scene of Teen Killing." *Los Angeles Sentinel,* April 11.

Moore, C. W. 1996. *The Mediation Process.* San Francisco: Jossey-Bass.

Morris, Aldon D., and Carol McClurg Mueller. 1992. *Frontiers in Social Movement Theory.* New Haven, Conn.: Yale University Press.

Morrison, Pat. 1990. "L.A. vs. O.C.: Just How Different Are They?" *Los Angeles Times Magazine,* June 17.

Morrissey, Marietta. 1983. "Ethnic Stratification and the Study of Chicanos." *Journal of Ethnic Studies,* Winter, pp. 71–99.

Multicultural Collaborative. 1996. "Race, Power, and Promise in Los Angeles: An Assessment of Responses to Human Relations Conflict." Los Angeles: Multicultural Collaborative.

Munoz, Carlos, Jr., and Charles P. Henry. 1990. "Coalition Politics in San Antonio and Denver: The Cisneros and Pena Mayoral Campaigns." In Rufus P. Browning, Dale Rogers Marshall, and David H. Tabb, eds., *Racial Politics in American Cities*. New York: Longman.

Murray, Charles. 1985. *Losing Ground: American Social Policy, 1950–1980*. New York: Basic Books.

Mydans, Seth. 1990. "For Them, Racial Harmony Is Work." *New York Times*, May 27.

Myrdal, Gunnar. 1944. *An American Dilemma: The Negro Problem and Modern Democracy*. New York: Harper.

Nader, L. 1993. "When Is Popular Justice Popular?" In S. E. Merry and N. Milner, eds., *The Possibility of Popular Justice*. Ann Arbor: University of Michigan Press.

Naison, Mark. 1983. *The Communists in Harlem during the Depression*. Champaign-Urbana: University of Illinois Press.

Nakanishi, Don T. 1991. "The Next Swing Vote? Asian Pacific Americans and California Politics." In Byran O. Jackson and Michael B. Preston, eds., *Racial and Ethnic Politics in California*. Berkeley, Calif.: Institute for Governmental Studies.

———. 1993. "Surviving Democracy's 'Mistake': Japanese Americans & the Enduring Legacy of Executive Order 9066." *Amerasia Journal* 19 (1): 7–35.

Nakano, Erich. 1993. "Building Common Ground—The Liquor Store Controversy." In Edward T. Chang and Russell C. Leong, eds., *Los Angeles-Struggles toward Multiethnic Community*. Seattle: University of Washington Press.

Navarro, Armando. 1993. "South Central Los Angeles Eruption: A Latino Perspective." In Edward T. Chang and Russell C. Leong, eds., *Los Angeles—Struggles toward Multiethnic Community*. Seattle: University of Washington Press.

———. 1997. *The Last Plantation: Color, Conflict, and Identity: Reflections of a New World Black*. Boston: Houghton Mifflin.

Njeri, Itabari. 1993. "The Conquest of Hate." *Los Angeles Times Magazine* April 25.

———. 1997. *The Last Plantation: Color, Conflict, and Identity: Reflections of a New World Black*. Boston: Houghton Mifflin.

Norman, Alex. 1992. "Black-Korean Relations: From Desperation to Dialogue, or From Shouting and Shooting to Sitting and Talking." Paper presented at the Black-Korean Encounter: Toward Understanding and Alliance Conference, California State University at Los Angeles.

Odendaal, A., and C. Spies. 1995. "Project Saamspan." *Track Two*, March–June.

Oh, Angela E. 1993. "Rebuilding Los Angeles: One Year Later or Why I Did Not Join RLA." In Edward T. Chang and Russell C. Leong, eds., *Los Angeles—Struggles toward Multiethnic Community*. Seattle: University of Washington Press.

Oh, David. 1983. *An Analysis of the Korean Community in Mid-Wilshire Area: Part I and II*. Los Angeles: Office of Economic Opportunity, State of California.

Oliver, Melvin, and David M. Grant. 1995. "Making Space for Multiethnic Coalitions: The Prospects for Coalition Politics in Los Angeles." In Eui-Young Yu and Edward T. Chang, eds., *Multiethnic Coalition Building in Los Angeles*. Los Angeles: Institute for Asian American and Pacific American Studies, California State University at Los Angeles. Distributed by Regina Books, Claremont, Calif.

Oliver, Melvin L., and James H. Johnson Jr. 1984. "Interethnic Conflict in An Urban Ghetto: The Case of Blacks and Latinos in Los Angeles." *Research in Social Movements, Conflict and Change* 6: 57–94.

Omatsu, Glenn. 1995. "Labor Organizing in Los Angeles: Confronting the Boundaries of Race and Ethnicity." In Eui-Young Yu and Edward T. Chang, eds., *Multiethnic Coalition Building in Los Angeles*. Los Angeles: Institute for Asian American and Pacific American Studies, California State University at Los Angeles.

Omi, Michael, and Howard Winant. 1986. *Racial Formation in the United States: From 1960s to the 1980s*. New York: Routledge & Kegan Paul.

———. 1993. *Racial Formation in the United States: From the 1960s to the 1990s*. Rev. ed. New York: Routledge.

Ong, Paul. 1993. "Poverty and Employment Issues in the Inner Urban Core." In A. J. Scott and E. R. Brown, eds., *South Central Los Angeles: Anatomy of an Urban Crisis*. Los Angeles: Lewis Center for Regional Policy Studies, University of California, June.

———, ed. 1994. *The State of Asian Pacific America: Economic Diversity, Issues & Politics*. A Public Policy Report. Los Angeles: LEAP Asian Pacific American Public Policy Institute and UCLA Asian American Studies Center.

Ong, Paul, and Suzanne Hee. 1993. "Losses in the Los Angeles Civil Unrest, April 29–May 1, 1992: Lists of the Damaged Properties and the L.A. Riot/Rebellion and Korean Merchants." Los Angeles: Center for Pacific Rim Studies, UCLA.

Ong, Paul, Janette R. Lawrence, and Kevin Davidson. 1992. *Pluralism and Residential Patterns in Los Angeles*. Los Angeles: Graduate School of Architecture and Urban Planning, University of California.

Ong, Paul, Kye Young Park, and Yasmin Tong. 1994. "The Korean-Black Conflict and the State." In Paul Ong, Edna Bonacich, and Lucie Cheng, eds., *The New Asian Immigration in Los Angeles and Global Restructuring*. Philadelphia: Temple University Press.

Ong, Paul, et al. 1989. *The Widening Divide: Income Inequality and Poverty in Los Angeles*. Los Angeles: Graduate School of Architecture and Urban Planning, University of California.

Osajima, Keith. 1988. "Asian Americans as the Model Minority: An Analysis of the Popular Press Image in the 1960s and 1980s." In Gary Okihiro et al., eds., *Reflections on Shattered Windows*. Pullman: Washington State University Press.

Park, Kye Young. 1995/96. "The Morality of a Commodity: A Case Study of 'Rebuilding L.A. without Liquor Stores.'" *Amerasia Journal* 21 (3): 1–24.

Park, Kye Young. 1997. *The Korean American Dream: Immigrants and Small Business in New York City.* Ithaca, N.Y.: Cornell University Press.

Pastor, Manuel. 1993. *Latinos and the Los Angeles Uprising: The Economic Context.* Claremont, Calif.: Tomas Rivera Center.

Patterson, Wayne. 1987. *The Korean Frontier in Hawaii: Immigration to Hawaii, 1896–1910.* Honolulu: University of Hawaii Press.

Peller, Gary. 1990. "Race Consciousness." *Duke Law Journal* (September): 758–847.

People for the American Way. 1992. *Democracy's Next Generation: A Study of American Youth on Race.* Washington, D.C.: People for the American Way.

Perlmutter, Philip. 1992. *Divided We Fall: A History of Ethnic, Religious, and Racial Prejudice in America.* Ames: Iowa State University Press.

Perlmutter, Nathan, and Ann Perlmutter. 1982. *The Real Anti-Semitism in America.* New York: Arbor House.

Pettigrew, Thomas. 1964. *A Profile of the Negro American.* Princeton, N.J.: Van Nostrand.

Phillips, Gary. 1993. "Specific Intent." *CrossRoads* 32 (June): 24–27.

Phillips, Kevin. 1991. *The Politics of Rich and Poor: Wealth and the American Electorate in the Reagan Aftermath.* New York: Harper Perennial.

Pincus, Fred L., and Howard J. Ehrlich. 1994. *Race and Ethnic Conflict: Contending Views on Prejudice, Discrimination, and Ethnoviolence.* Boulder, Colo.: Westview Press.

Piven, Frances, and Richard A. Cloward. 1971. *Regulating the Poor: The Functions of Public Welfare.* New York: Vintage Books.

Portes, Alejandro, and Robert Bach. 1985. *Latin Journey: Cuban and Mexican Immigrants in the U.S.* Berkeley and Los Angeles: University of California Press.

Portes, Alejandro, and Saskia Sassen-Koob. 1987. "Making It Underground: Comparative Material on the Informal Sector in Western Market Economies." *American Journal of Sociology* 93 (1): 30–61.

Portes, Aljandro, and John Walton. 1981. *Labor, Class, and the International System.* New York: Academic Press.

Prillaid, David. 1995. "Development in Conflict—Conflict in Development." *Track Two* 4, nos. 1 and 2: 12–15.

Pruitt, D. G., and J. Z. Rubin. 1986. *Social Conflict: Escalation, Stalemate, and Settlement.* New York: Random House.

Purdum, Todd S. 1990a. "Angry Dinkins Defends Role in Race Cases." *New York Times,* May 9.

———. 1990b. "Judge Critical of Dinkins over Boycott." *New York Times,* May 11.

———. 1990c. "Dinkins Asks for Racial Unity and Offers to Mediate Boycott." *New York Times,* May 12.

———. 1990d. "Dinkins Supports Shunned Grocers." *New York Times,* September 22.

Rainey, James. 1993. "Council Opens Debate on Limited Legal Street Vending." *Los Angeles Times*, December 11.

Ramos, George. 1993. "Turning an Ear to Silent Latino Constituency." *Los Angeles Times*, May 3, 1993.

Ramos, George, and John H. Lee. 1991. "Demonstrators Demand That Korean Market Never Reopen." *Los Angeles Times*, March 22.

Ratnesar, Romesh. 1997. "The Next Big Divide?" *Time*, December 1.

Regalado, Jaime A. 1994. "Community Coalition Building." In Mark Baldassare, ed., *The Los Angeles Riots*. San Francisco: Westview Press.

———. 1995. "Creating Multiethnic Harmony?" In Eui-Young Yu and Edward T. Chang, eds., *Multiethnic Coalition Building in Los Angeles*. Los Angeles: Institute for Asian American and Pacific American Studies, California State University at Los Angeles.

Reich, Michael. 1981. *Racial Inequality*. Princeton, N.J.: Princeton University Press.

Reiss, A. J., and H. E. Aldrich. 1971. "Absentee Ownership and Management in the Black Ghetto: Social and Economic Consequences." *Social Problems* 18 (3): 319–39.

Report of the National Advisory Commission on Civil Disorders. 1968. Washington, D.C., March 1.

Riker, W. H. 1962. *The Theory of Political Coalitions*. New Haven, Conn.: Yale University Press.

Rivera, Carla. 1992. "Korean-American Looking Elsewhere after Riots." *Los Angeles Times*, December 24.

Rodriguez, Irma, and Graciela Vasquez-Rodriguez. 1993. "Pico-Union: A Zone of Need." Master's thesis, University of California at Los Angeles.

Roediger, David R. 1991. *The Wages of Whiteness: Race and the Making of the American Working Class*. London: Verso.

Rubenstein, Richard E., and Robert M. Fogelson, eds. 1969. *Mass Violence in America: The Los Angeles Riots*. New York: Arno Press.

Saito, Leland T. 1993. "Asian Americans and Latinos in San Gabriel Valley, California: Interethnic Political Cooperation and Redistricting 1990–92." In Edward T. Chang and Russell C. Leong, eds., 1994. *Los Angeles—Struggles toward Multiethnic Community*. Seattle: University of Washington Press.

Sassen-Koob, Saskia. 1982. "Recomposition and Peripheralization at the Core." In Marlene Dixon and Susanne Jonas, eds., *The New Normads*. San Francisco: Synthesis Publications.

———. 1991. *The Global City: New York, London, Tokyo*. Princeton, N.J.: Princeton University Press.

Schaefer, Richard T. 1987. "Social Distance of Black College Students at a Predominantly White University." *Sociology and Social Research* 72 (October): 30–32.

Schlager, Edella. 1995. "Policy Making and Collective Action: Defining Coalitions within the Advocacy Coalition Framework." *Policy Sciences* 29: 243–70.

Schlesinger, Arthur M., Jr. 1991. *The Disuniting of America: Reflection on a Multicultural Society*. Knoxville, Tenn.: Whittle Books.

Scott, A. J., and E. R. Brown, eds. 1993. *South Central Los Angeles: Anatomy of an Urban Crisis*. Los Angeles: Lewis Center for Regional Policy Studies, University of California, June.

Sheppard, Harold L. 1947. "The Negro Merchant: A Study of Negro Anti-Semitism." *Journal of Sociology* 53 (September): 96–99.

Shorris, Earl. 1982. "The Jews of the New Right." *The Nation*, May 8, pp. 557–61.

Sims, Calvin. 1990. "Black Customers, Korean Grocers: Need and Mistrust." *New York Times*, May 17.

Sitkoff, Harvard. 1981. *The Struggle for Black Equality, 1954–1980*. New York: Hill & Wang.

———. 1992. "Inside Exopolis: Scenes from Orange County." In Michael Sorkin, ed., *Variations on a Theme Park: The New American City and the End of Public Space*. New York: Noonday Press.

Soja, Edward W. 1989. *Postmodern Geographies: The Reassertion of Space in Critical Social Theory*. New York: Verso.

Sonenshein, Raphael J. 1989. "The Dynamics of Biracial Coalitions: Crossover Politics in Los Angeles." *Western Political Quarterly* 42 (June): 333–53.

———. 1993. *Politics in Black and White: Race and Power in Los Angeles*. Princeton, N.J.: Princeton University Press.

Sowell, Thomas. 1980. *Ethnic America*. New York: Basic Books.

Special Advisor to the Board of Police Commissioners on the Civil Disorder in Los Angeles. 1992. *A Report: The City in Crisis*. Los Angeles, October 21.

Stack, Carol B. 1974. *All Our Kin: Strategies for Survival in a Black Community*. New York: Harper & Row.

Stansbury, Jeff. 1989. "L.A. Labor & the New Immigrants." *Labor Research Review*, no. 13.

Stein, M. L. 1992a. "Coverage Complaints." *Editor & Publisher*, May 23.

———. 1992b. "Politicians to Examine Media." *Editor & Publisher*, July 25.

———. 1992c. "Coverage Questioned Again." *Editor & Publisher*, August 1.

Stewart, Ella. 1989. "Ethnic Cultural Diversity: Ethnographic Study of Cultural Study of Cultural Differences and Communication Styles between Korean Merchants and African American Patrons in South Los Angeles." Master's thesis, California State University at Los Angeles.

———. 1994. "Communication between African Americans and Korean Americans: Before and after the Los Angeles Riots." In Edward T. Chang and Russell C. Leong, eds., *Los Angeles—Struggles toward Multiethnic Community*. Seattle: University of Washington Press.

Stolte, John F. 1990. "Power Processes in Structures of Dependence and Exchange." *Advances in Group Process* 7: 129–50.

Stone, Chuck. 1968. *Black Political Power in America.* New York: Bobbs-Merrill.

Sunoo, Harold Hakwon, and Sonia Shin Sunoo. 1977. "The Heritage of the First Korean Women Immigrants in the United States, 1903–1924." *Korean Christian Journal,* Spring, pp. 142–71.

Sunoo, Sonia. 1978. "Korean Women Pioneers of the Pacific Northwest." *Oregon Historical Quarterly* 79: 51–64.

Takaki, Ronald. 1989. *Strangers from a Different Shore: A History of Asian Americans.* New York: Penguin Books.

Tedlin, Kent L., and Richard W. Murray. 1994. "Support for Biracial Political Coalitions among Blacks and Hispanics." *Social Science Quarterly* 75 (December): 772–89.

Terry, Don. 1990. "Hynes Criticized in Report on Boycott." *New York Times,* August 31.

Terkel, Studs. 1993. *Race: How Blacks & Whites Think & Feel about the American Obsession.* New York: Anchor Books.

Tierney, William G. 1993. *Building Communities of Difference.* Westport, Conn.: Bergin & Garvey.

Tobas, Hector. 1990. "Latinos Transform South Los Angeles." *Los Angeles Times,* February 16.

Tomas Rivera Institute. 1997. "Diversifying the Los Angeles Area Latino Mosaic: Salvadoran and Guatemalan Leaders' Assessment of Community Public Policy Needs." Claremont, Calif.: Tomas Rivera Institute.

Tong, Yasmin Theresa. 1992. "In the Middle: Mediating Black-Korean Conflict in South Central Los Angeles." Master's thesis, University of California at Los Angeles.

Torres, Andres. 1995. *Between Melting Pot and Mosaic: African Americans and Puerto Ricans in the New York Political Economy.* Philadelphia: Temple University Press.

Totten, George O., III, and H. Eric Schockman, eds. 1994. *Community in Crisis: The Korean American Community after the Los Angeles Civil Unrest of April 1992.* Los Angeles: Center for Multiethnic and Transnational Studies, University of Southern California.

Tsukashima, Ronald. 1986. "A Test of Competing Contact Hypothesis in the Study of Black Anti-Semitic Beliefs." In Arnold Dashefsky, ed., *Contemporary Jewry.* Vol. 7. New Brunswick, NJ: Transaction.

Tucker, Curtis R., Jr. (Tucker Committee). 1992. *To Rebuild Is Not Enough: Final Report and Recommendations of the Assembly Special Committee on the Los Angeles Crisis,* Sacramento, September 28.

Uhlaner, Carole J. 1991. "Perceived Discrimination and Prejudice and the Coalitions Prospects of Blacks, Latinos and Asian Americans." In Byran O. Jackson and Michael B. Preston, eds., *Racial and Ethnic Politics in California*. Berkeley, Calif.: IGS Press.

Underwood, Katherine. 1997. "Ethnicity Is Not Enough: Latino-Led Multiracial Coalitions in Los Angeles." *Urban Affairs Review* 33 (September): 3–27.

United Asian Women of California, ed. 1989. *Making Waves: An Anthology of Writings by and about Asian American Women*. Boston: Beacon Press.

Waldinger, Roger, and Mehdi Bozorgmehr, eds. 1986. *Ethnic Los Angeles*. New York: Russell Sage.

Waldinger, Roger David. 1993. *The Ethnic Enclave Debate Revisited*. Working Paper no. 249, Institute of Industrial Relations, University of California at Los Angeles.

Waldinger, Roger David, and Mehdi Bozorgmehr, eds. 1996. *Ethnic Los Angeles*. New York: Russell Sage Foundation.

Waldinger, Roger David, et al. 1990. *Ethnic Entrepreneurs: Immigrant Business in Industrial Societies*. Newbury Park, Calif.: Sage.

Wallerstein, Immanuel. 1974. *The Modern World-System*. New York: Academic Press.

Weisbord, Robert, and Arthur Stein. 1970. *Bitter Sweet Encounter: The AfroAmerican and the American Jews*. Westport, Conn.: Negro University Press.

Wellman, David. 1984. *Portraits of White Racism*. Cambridge: Cambridge University Press.

West, Cornell. 1993. *Race Matters*. Boston: Beacon Press.

Wilke, Henk A. 1985. *Coalition Formation*. Amsterdam: Elsevier.

Williams, Brackette F. 1989. "A Class Act: Anthropology and the Race to Nation Across Ethnic Terrain." *Annual Review of Anthropology* 18: 401–44.

Wilson, William Julius. 1978. *The Declining Significance of Race*. Chicago: University of Chicago Press.

———. 1987. *Truly Disadvantaged: The Inner City, the Underclass, and Public Policy*. Chicago: University of Chicago Press.

Wong, Charles. 1977. "Blacks and Chinese Grocery Stores in L.A.'s Black Ghetto." *Urban Life* 5 (4): 439–64.

Yoon, In-Jin. 1997. *On My Own: Korean Businesses and Race Relations in America*. Chicago: University of Chicago Press.

Young, Philip K. Y. 1983. "Family Labor, Sacrifice, and Competition: Korean Greengrocers in New York City." *Amerasia Journal* 10 (2): 53–72.

———. 1990. *Korean Community Profile: Life and Consumer Patterns*. Los Angeles: *Korea Times* / Hankook Ilbo.

Yu, Eui-Young. 1983. "Korean Communities in America: Past, Present, and Future." *Amerasia Journal* 10 (2): 23–51.

———. 1990. *Korean Community Profile: Life and Consumer Patterns*. Los Angeles: *Korea Times*.

————. 1994. *Black-Korean Encounter: Toward Understanding and Alliance.* Los Angeles: Institute for Asian American and Pacific Asian Studies, California State University at Los Angeles.

Yu, Eui-Young, and Edward T. Chang, eds. 1995. *Multiethnic Coalition Building in Los Angeles.* Los Angeles: Institute for Asian American and Pacific American Studies, California State University at Los Angeles.

Yu, Eui-Young, Eun-Sik Yang, and Earl Philip, eds. 1982. *Koreans in Los Angeles.* Los Angeles: Koryo Research Institute.

Yu, Jin H. 1980. *The Korean Merchants in the Black Community.* Elkins Park, Pa.: Philip Jaisohn Foundation.

Yung, Judith. 1995. *Unbound Feet: A Social History of Chinese Women in San Francisco.* Berkeley and Los Angeles: University of California Press.

Zenner, W. 1982. "Arabic-Speaking Immigrants in North America as Middleman Minorities." *Ethnic and Racial Studies* 5: 457–77.

Zhou, Min. 1992. *Chinatown: The Socioeconomic Potential of an Urban Enclave.* Philadelphia: Temple University Press.

Zia, Helen. 1993. "Women of Color in Leadership." *Social Policy,* Summer, pp. 51–55.

Zimmer, Catherine, and Howard Aldrich. 1987. "Resource Mobilization through EthnicNetwork." *Sociological Perspectives* 30 (October): 422–45.

Zukin, Sharon. 1992. *Landscapes of Power: From Detroit to Disney World.* Berkeley and Los Angeles: University of California Press.

Index

Advocacy: vs. dialogue, 123–124; in mediation, 132–134

African Americans: deindustrialization and, 27–28; and demographic change in Los Angeles, 1, 12, 17; economic development of, 50–51; history of, in Los Angeles, 13–17; history of violence and, 140; and Jews, 53–55; and Korean Americans. *See* Black-Korean Alliance; Korean–African American relations; and Latinos. *See* Latino–African American relations; Latino-Black Roundtable (LBR); nationalism of, 52–53, 64–65, 73; 1992 Los Angeles civil unrest, view of, 4, 143n1. *See also* 1992 Los Angeles civil unrest; and other racial groups, 17, 46t, 46–47; police brutality and, 29–30, 68–69; political power of, 119; U.S. riots of 1965 and, 15

Alternative dispute resolution, 131–134

Anti-Semitism, among African Americans, 53–54

Asian Americans: media invisibility of, 61–62; in Pico-Union, 84; political participation of, in Los Angeles, 17; population increase in Los Angeles, 4, 11–12; and Rodney King verdicts, 62; in southern California, 3–4, 13; in U.S. racial policy, 11; *See also* Korean Americans

Asian Pacific Dispute Resolution Center, 65, 133

Asians, Southeast, Refugee Act of 1981 and, 73

Bakewell, Danny, 64; and John's Market shooting, 74; *Los Angeles Times* coverage of, 72, 79

Bakke decision, and racial tension, 28

Bensonhurst incident, 68, 70

Bilingual education, and Latino-Black Roundtable, 122

BKA. *See* Black-Korean Alliance

Black Employees Association, membership in Latino-Black Roundtable (LBR), 113

Black-Korean Alliance (BKA): code of ethics developed by, 114, 118, 119, 123; creation of, 34, 65, 112; cross-cultural dynamics in, 122–123; dialogue model for, limits of, 123–124, 139; dissolution of, 109, 115–123, 126–127; and diversity in Korean and black communities, 124–126; events sponsored by, 114; goals of, 34, 108, 112; Harlins-Du case and, 74, 121; lack of resources, 115–116; limitations of, 124–125, 139; mayor's office and, 76, 115–116; membership of, 113, 116–120; nationalism and ethnic solidarity in, 120–122; organizational structure of, 113; survey of, 112–128; survey of, methodology in, 106–107

Black nationalism: in Korean–African American conflict, 52–53, 73; Los Angeles vs. New York, 64–65

Black power movement, and coalition building, 108–109

Black-white paradigm: in analysis of 1992 Los Angeles civil unrest, 5; of race, 2–3, 11–12

Boycotts, of Korean stores: black nationalism and, 53, 64–65; Church Fruit boycott, 76, 145n3, 145n4; John's Market boycott, 74, 116; in Los Angeles, 33, 48; in New York, 33; in New York vs. Los Angeles, 64–65; Red Apple boycott, 65–66, 68–71, 75–76; Sonny Carson and, 66, 73

Bradley, Mayor Tom: and Latasha Harlins shooting, 74, 75–76; vs. Mayor Ed Koch, 65

Brotherhood Crusade, 72; and Du verdict, 34; and John's Market shooting, 74

California: migration of nonwhites to, 13–15; race relations in, 3–4; *See also* Los Angeles

171

About the Authors

Edward T. Chang is an associate professor of ethnic studies and a former director of the Center for Asian Pacific America at the University of California at Riverside.

Jeannette Diaz-Veizades is an executive faculty member at the Saybrook Graduate School, where she teaches research methods as well as courses in psychology and in community, social, and institutional change.